First Nations Teachers

Identity and Community, Struggle and Change

June Beynon

Deborah Brown, Marilyn Bryant, Pansy Collison,
Cameron Hill, Eva-Ann Hill, Isabel Hill, Maureen LaGroix,
Nadine Leighton, Beatrice Skog, and Mel Tait

First Nations teachers :
identity and community, struggle and change
© 2008 June Benyon

Library And Archives Canada Cataloging in Publication
Benyon, June
First Nations teachers : identity and community, struggle and change / June Benyon.

Includes bibliographical references.
ISBN 978-1-55059-349-5

1. Indians of North America--Education--Canada.
2. Aboriginal Canadian teachers.
3. Aboriginal Canadian teachers--Biography.
I. Title.

E96.2.B45 2008   371.829'97071   C2008-900767-0

210 1220 Kensington Rd NW   p. 403-283-0900
Calgary, Ab. T2N 3P5   f. 403-283-6945
www.temerondetselig.com DETSELIG   e. temeron@telusplanet.net
ENTERPRISES LTD

We recognize the support of the Government of Canada through the Book Publishing Industry Development Program (BPIDP) for our publishing program.
We also acknowledge the support of the Alberta Foundation for the Arts for our publishing program.

COMMITTED TO THE DEVELOPMENT OF CULTURE AND THE ARTS

SAN 113-0234
ISBN 978-155059-349-5
Printed in Canada

Cover Design by James Dangerous

TABLE OF CONTENTS

CHAPTER 3
LOOKING TO THE PAST: SOURCES OF INDIGENOUS EDUCATIONAL DISCOURSES

CHAPTER 4
RESISTING COLONIAL DISCOURSES OF THE FEDERAL GOVERNMENT AND CHURCHES

CHAPTER 5
ON THE THRESHOLD OF CHANGE: STRUGGLES BETWEEN DISCOURSES OF INDIGENOUS EDUCATIONAL REFORM AND MAINSTREAM DISCOURSES

CHAPTER 6
THE WORLD OF EMPLOYMENT: FINDING A JOB   79

CHAPTER 7
COMMUNITIES AND PARENTS   97

CHAPTER 8
SCHOOLS AND CLASSROOMS;
COLLEAGUES AND KIDS

ACKNOWLEDGEMENTS

We are enormously grateful to the Vancouver Foundation (Van Dusen Foundation) for their generous financial support of this book. Similarly, this project would not have been possible if we had not had the strong institutional support of the First Nations Education Council of School District #52, Prince Rupert. The Simon Fraser University Publications Fund substantially contributed to bringing this book to print.

From the outset of this project, Dr. Lorna Williams – formerly Director of Aboriginal Education for the Province of BC, and currently Canada Research Chair at the University of Victoria – encouraged and guided the process, and reinforced the importance of pursuing the book to its completion. Lorna also provided valuable editorial input at various stages in the development of the manuscript. Dr. Kelleen Toohey of the Faculty of Education at SFU provided supportive and insightful editorial assistance as well. For her patient work of copy editing on short timelines, Barbara Johnston is much appreciated.James Dangerous of Detselig did deft and elegant work on final editing, layout, and graphics.

Once all of the vignettes were collected, Janice Grout provided invaluable assistance in organizing the vignettes thematically. Thanks are also extended to Tammy Blumhagen for her work compiling and summarizing School Board minutes. We appreciate the help of School District #52 in facilitating her work. Our appreciation is extended to John Corsiglia and Christine Blanche Stewart for compiling and summarizing Department of Indian Affairs documents. British Columbia provincial archivists Tanya Culback and Jay Gilbert were most helpful, as was archivist Wendy Incell at the Union of BC Indian Chiefs.

Finally, we are especially grateful and appreciative to Debbie Leighton-Stephens – the District Principal of First Nations Education School District #52 – for her unfailing support, encouragement, and guidance. Our gratitude and thanks also go to Frank Leighton-Stephens for the photo on the cover of the book, and to Sam Bryant for the cover motif of the boat surrounded by four clan crests, representing and celebrating the teacher's shared journey.

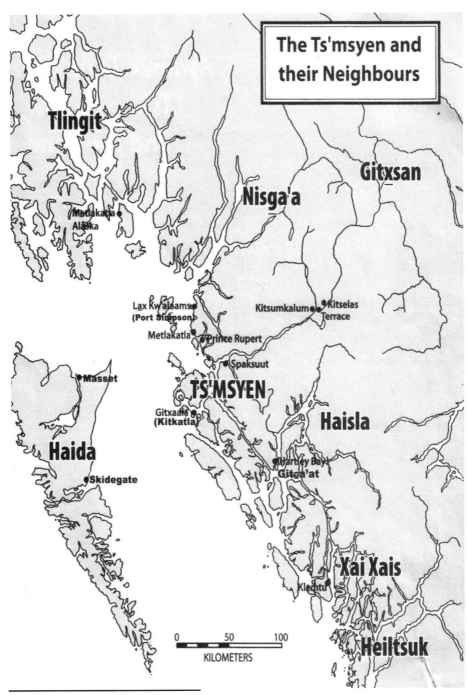

Map: Campbell, 2005, p 32

INTRODUCTION

Reflecting on her position as a First Nations teacher, Pansy Collison said:

> I think [that as a teacher of Haida ancestry] I have a lot to contribute to students, regardless of their age or grade, because I am genuinely concerned about our culture. I think I've got a really good rapport with the students. They see me as a native person, and come up to me automatically. It's just easier for them to approach me because I am native. They don't have any second thoughts. I can understand their environment: where they came from. I can feel some of the struggles that their parents went through, and after I get to know them, I can help out more. If there's a problem with anything – health, lack of food – I can easily talk to them. I guess there is automatic sensitivity to me. They are able to see who I am, that I am a teacher, and that I can help them.

Pansy is one of nine First Nations teachers from the Prince Rupert and Haida Gwaii school districts in north coastal British Columbia, Canada, whose experiences as educators are at the heart of this book. Her statement illustrates a central principle from the landmark policy document Indian Control of Indian Education (1972)[1] that:

> [Indian] teachers...who have an intimate understanding of Indian traditions, psychology, way of life and language . . . are best able to create the learning environment suited to the habits and interests of the Indian child.

National Indian Brotherhood, 1972

1 Abele, Dittburner & Graham (2000) identify a succession of terms used in official Canadian documents starting with "native" and "Indian" in the 1970s and superceded, but not replaced by "Aboriginal," and "First Nations." In part, these terms reflect government efforts to position diverse cultures and languages into a single legal

In response to this idea, teacher education institutions across Canada developed a variety of approaches to preparing teachers who would be centrally positioned to work toward re-establishing control of education for their own children (Battiste, 1995; Gardner, 2000; Hampton, 2000; Kirkness, 1999; Williams & Wyatt, 1987). Yet there is scant documentation of how the varied experiences of these teachers' lives and work compare to the vision of "Indian control" outlined in policy. If First Nations teachers are key in educational reform how might they go about bringing desired changes? How might their unique educational histories and experiences with First Nations languages and cultures be implicated in their professional practices? The vignettes collected here, narrated and written by

framework. In contemporary Canada, "First Nations" is a common term of reference in official documents. It responds to the need for a collective term that encompasses the large number of distinct linguistic and cultural groups in the country, and to acknowledge their distinct political status. Starting in 1982, when the Assembly of First Nations succeeded the National Indian Brotherhood ("Assembly of First Nations," n.d.) it became widely used as the prominent organization representing the interests of Métis and Inuit as well as Indians. "Aboriginal" is used in the Canadian Constitution Act to encompass First Nations, Inuit and Métis. The Royal Commission on Aboriginal Peoples (1997) contributed to the prominence of this usage.

"Indigenous" is another collective term referring to Aboriginal peoples both in Canada and other nation states where colonization has occurred. The consistent use of "Indigenous" as a global term of reference is reinforced by the work of the World Council of Indigenous Populations, which dates to the UN Commission on Human Rights (Battiste & Henderson, 2000, p. 2). Collections of writings about teaching and learning often employ the term "Indigenous" because they feature works from many nation states. This usage also signals underlying similarities in ways of learning and teaching of diverse and widely dispersed linguistic and cultural groups. The term "Indigenous" emerged from the American Indian Movement and the Canadian Indian Brotherhood in the 1970s. Smith states, "The term has enabled the collective voices of colonized people to be expressed strategically in the international arena. It has also been an umbrella enabling communities and peoples to come together, transcending their own colonized contexts and experiences, in order to learn, share, plan, organize and struggle collectively for self-determination on the global and local stages" (1999, p. 7). This book will use the specific linguistic (Sm'algyax) and cultural (Ts'msyen and Haida) affiliations to honor the identities and uniqueness of these nations.

Marilyn Bryant, Pansy Collison, Cameron Hill, Eva-Ann Hill, Isabelle Hill, Nadine Leighton, Beatrice Skog, Mel Tait, (Prince Rupert school district) Deborah Brown, and Maureen LaGroix (Haida Gwaii school district) provide valuable insights regarding these questions. Short biographies of each teacher appear in Appendix I.

The vignettes illustrate key challenges of developing First Nations control where students of First Nations ancestries comprise the majority of district enrollments.[2] They embody the rapport that these teachers have with their students. They also illustrate other key points that Pansy identifies in the opening to this introductory chapter, namely that teachers are concerned about their students' cultures, that they are familiar with the environments they live in, and that they share some of their parents' struggles.

The teachers were classmates during the five-year, full-time Prince Rupert/Simon Fraser University First Nations Language and Culture Teacher Education Program. Initiated by the Prince Rupert First Nations Education Council, it was jointly endorsed and supported in varied ways by the Prince Rupert School District and the University of Northern British Columbia. As a member of the Faculty of Education at Simon Fraser University, I represented the faculty in the process of constructing the program. While I had taught other cohorts of First Nations student teachers in Prince Rupert,[3] I had no supervisory relationship with these ten teachers. All course work and practica in this five-year program took place in the city of Prince Rupert, the present day regional centre of the Ts'msyen nation.[4] It was designed to include Ts'msyen culture

---

2 Enrollments of First Nations are variable from school to school. Village school enrollments are nearly 100% First Nations, individual schools in the city of Prince Rupert range anywhere from 30 to 60%, reflecting neighborhood demographics.

3 Prince Rupert is 1500 kilometers by road from Vancouver and approximately ninety minutes by air.

4 Ts'msyen is the name of the north coastal First Nations people. The literal translation is "people inside the Skeena." (Campbell, K., 2005, p. 10) The Skeena is a main regional river and flows out from the interior to the coast at Prince Rupert.

and Sm'algyax language[5] as an integral part of professional training.[6]

Beginning in 1995, immediately after they completed the program, and for the ensuing ten years I met annually – and occasionally twice a year - with the graduates to share their stories of seeking and gaining employment, teaching in varied school and community settings, furthering their studies through graduate work, and constructing learning environments that could effectively engage diverse First Nations learners in a spectrum of classrooms and schools.[7] The transcripts of our tape-recorded sessions provided many of the narratives, from which the vignettes in this book were drawn. The remaining vignettes are first hand accounts that participants selected to put into writing. These stories are central to this book, and provide insights into their dilemmas and struggles and tell of how they went about taking action to resolve them. Appendix 2, on research methodology, outlines details of our collaborative relationships in the construction of this book.

---

5 Sm'algyax is the language spoken by the Ts'msyen living along the coast. Pronunciation of some Sm'algyax words and place names are available online at *http://www.sd52.bc.ca/fnes/sf1.html*. A pronunciation guide is also available in Campbell, 2005, 236-237. Since Sm'algyax first appeared in writing, there has been considerable variation in both the orthographies and spellings. This book employs the most recent spellings, based on the works of the Sm'algyax language teachers and the linguist John Dunn. In particular, spellings of place names are taken from Campbell, 2005. This book uses these spellings, except when quoting or referencing sources that use other spellings, in which cases the spellings used in the referenced sources will be retained.

6 Limited program resources prevented the offering of courses in Haida language.

7 The Northcoast Tribal Council, School District #52 and Simon Fraser University also jointly sponsored a master's program entitled Curriculum and Instruction in First Nations Education based in Prince Rupert. This program enrolled educators of First Nations and other ancestries.

TAKING A THEORETICAL PERSPECTIVE

This book brings together ideas from liberatory pedagogy (Chapter 1), Indigenous pedagogical theories of identity, teaching, and learning (elaborated in Chapters 1, 2, and 3), and socio cultural theories on identity, power, and change (introduced in Chapters 1 and 2). These mutually supportive perspectives explain how the struggles and identities of educators are rich resources for transforming colonial and postcolonial educational systems. They provide suggestions for how these teachers resourcefully built from Indigenous ideologies and practices, as well as from the world of mainstream schools in order to construct their own identities. They also emphasize that struggles to construct identity, far from being individual efforts, in fact connect us to others. These struggles and connections fuel the transformation of colonial educational systems into spaces that support and encourage Indigenous learners.

TAKING A HISTORICAL PERSPECTIVE

The experiences of the teachers set forth in this collection are connected to both the broad history of Aboriginal education in Canada, as well as to the specific history of north coastal British Columbia (pre-colonial, colonial, and post-colonial). This history, outlined in Chapters 4 and 5, illustrates the obstacles and dilemmas that Freire (1970) referred to as the "limiting situations" that we *can* alter (italics mine). In struggles with the legacy of this history, First Nations teachers have initiated the process of educational transformation. The vignettes in this collection illustrate these struggles; they also illustrate the enthusiasm, creativity, and accomplishments that were born from them.

The chapters in which the vignettes appear (2, 6, 7, 8, and 9) are chronologically arranged to reflect the ten-year period over which they were collected. Predictably, the earlier vignettes are filled with the struggles and dilemmas of finding a job, being a new teacher, and juggling community and professional expectations. Throughout this time, teachers were also engaged in the challenges and excitement of creating new curriculum and language programs. Their tremendous productivity and innovation is most fully reflected in Chapter 9.

CHAPTER 1:
PERSPECTIVES ON CHANGE

In order . . . to be able to wage the struggle for their liberation, [people] must perceive the reality of oppression not as a closed world from which there is no exit, but as a limiting situation which they can transform.

(Freire, 1970, p. 34)

Difficult circumstances, obstacles created by formal institutional policies and procedures, as well as historical acts of oppression and informal institutional norms – or "the way things have always been done around here" – stand in opposition to teachers' possibilities for improving both their students' and their own learning and teaching. How then do Indigenous teachers take action (Freire, 1970; Holland, Lachicotte, Skinner, & Cain, 1998) and improvise (Holland, et al., 1998) innovative practices that renegotiate and redress long standing colonial and postcolonial historical educational practices that have repressed and marginalized their people? How do these teachers operate as agents for educational and social change?

LIBERATORY PEDAGOGY

Liberatory pedagogy that addresses issues of agency and power (Brant-Castellano, 2000; Freire,1970; Holland et al., 1998) is a rich source for both the development of human agency and for the crafting of change in educational and social settings with histories of oppression. Discourse and dialogue (Bakhtin, 1981; Freire,1970; Holland et al. 1998); story (Anderson, 2000; Anderson & Lawrence, 2003; Davies & Harré, 1999); and identity (Anderson, 2000; Hall, 1996; Holland et. al. 1988; hooks, 1994) are also powerful tools in dismantling oppressive conditions and reshaping them in hopeful ways.

Based on his long term work in adult literacy, Paulo Freire (1970) identified education as a tool for bringing liberation/agency to people who have suffered political and social oppression. In Canada, as in many other nations, formal schooling was a colonial tool for the domination of Aboriginal peoples; hence the theory of employing education as a tool for liberation is replete with contradictions. The *Report of the Royal Commission on Aboriginal Peoples*, which addresses concerns of First Nations, Inuit, and Métis, acknowledges this paradox:

> Despite the painful experiences that Aboriginal people carry with them from formal education systems, they still see education as the hope for the future, and they are determined to see education fulfill its promise.
>
> (1996, 3, p. 434)

Brant-Castellano, Davis, and Lahache theorize the importance of education in the history of Aboriginal political reform movements. They see education "at the heart of the struggle of Aboriginal peoples to regain control over their lives as communities and nations." (2000, p. xi)

How can the educational systems that have been used as tools of subjugation be used to reverse the oppression that they have created? Perspectives on agency and power, discourse and dialogue, and story and identity help in working through this paradox.

AGENCY AND POWER

> Human agency may be frail, especially among those with little power, but it happens daily and mundanely, and it deserves our attention.
>
> (Holland et al., 1998, p. 5)

Even in difficult circumstances, our abilities to direct our actions, and ways of thinking open possibilities for positive changes. We often find the tools for change in the oppressive systems themselves. As Holland et al. (1998) put it: "while 'alien' voices may position us, they also provide us with tools to reshape our positions" (p. 45).

Colonial school systems are prime examples of "alien voices." Many of the vignettes in this book and much of the historical documentation of schooling presented in Chapters 3 through 5 illustrate how the Ts'msyen Nation in British Columbia and Aboriginal communities across Canada disrupted the very educational systems designed to subjugate their cultures and languages, and employed these systems as a means for promoting their cultures and languages instead. Taking up the challenge to become a teacher in mainstream schools as a means to further Aboriginal language and culture is a powerful example of such agency.

DISCOURSE AND DIALOGUE

For Aboriginal teachers in Canada and Indigenous teachers in other nation states, the "alien" voices identified by Holland et al. (1998) are often articulated within the same colonial and postcolonial educational systems that have suppressed traditions of Aboriginal and Indigenous language, culture, and kinship. These "voices of authority" constitute "the official line" (Bakhtin, p. 1981, 344) that constitute both the "talk and text(s)"(Gillborn, 1995, p. 19). They are "words and the ways of using words" (Emerson & Holquist,1981, p. 427) articulated by government, schools, and places of worship. Bakhtin refers to these as "authoritative discourses." They work their way into our thinking and shape our writing and speech, often without our full awareness that this is happening.

Part of the authority of these official discourses (prohibitions against speaking traditional languages, requirements to use English, the outlawing of traditional ceremonial objects) is that, while initially alien and imposed, they can, through years of repetition, become an unquestioned part of daily life. If you have ever found yourself saying things to your own students or children and realized that you "sounded just like your parents," you may be hearing discourses that have been silent for long periods and that can be instantly and involuntarily revived. Marilyn, who performs with and coordinates the work of a group of Ts'msyen dancers and drummers, recounts how authoritative discourses of church and residential schools that prohibited the use of Sm'algya̱x and Haida languages became part of her parents' ways of thinking. In turn, as she states here, these prohibitions had significant effects on her.

> My grandparents were around when I was growing up, but they were really, really hesitant to teach us anything about their background. My parents thought that the White way was the right way, and that their own cultural ways were wrong. They wouldn't teach any of their kids the language. They both spoke Sm'algya̱x. They didn't want their kids knowing the language, because they couldn't use it in the White school and they wanted them educated in the White system . . . then my paternal grandmother, who taught the Haida language to others in the community, didn't teach that to their own children either.

Nevertheless, in spite of prohibitions and other powerful and conflicting authoritative discourses, including Sm'algya̱x and Haida narratives, family, and clan ceremonies were not completely supplanted. As we shall see in subsequent chapters, these remain a rich resource which teachers draw from in constructing their own "internally persuasive" discourses and teaching practices (Bakhtin, p. 342).

Internally persuasive discourses are diverse and unique, crafted out of struggles with the variety of discourses we encounter over the course of our lifetimes. In these discourses, we "tell things in our own words, with our own accents, gestures, and modifications" (Emerson & Holquist, 1981, p. 424). The vignettes in this book are a rich expression of the teachers' internally persuasive discourses.

Internally persuasive discourses are articulated in the intimate spaces of home and family. In the next chapter, which focuses on issues of identity, all of the teachers' vignettes refer to the importance of their families and homes in contributing to who they are. Internally persuasive discourses are also forged in more public spaces, in struggles with authoritative policy discourses, and with the internally persuasive discourses of colleagues, students, and parents.

Bakhtin theorizes that what we believe in, or what he calls our "ideological consciousness"(p. 348) is an outcome of struggling with diverse discourses. Struggle is certainly central to the experiences of First Nations educators working to reform Anglo-European authoritative discourses of church and government. The struggle entails disengaging from what has "ceased to mean," and creatively developing "ever newer ways to mean" (Bakhtin, p. 346).

Engaged in struggles with a variety of authoritative discourses during their lives and education, these teachers do, nevertheless, have opportunities to answer with internally persuasive discourses that articulate their unique histories, voices, identities, and points of view. The vignettes collected here reflect the struggles, how they see things in their worlds, and express them in their own words.

Possibilities for working through struggles in order to articulate our perspectives can be greatly supported by dialogue. Dialogue is only possible if we can hold more than one perspective at a time. While voicing our own ideas we engage with others' "competing definitions." (Emerson & Holquist, p. 427) In this reciprocal process, possibilities emerge for reshaping our ideas as we consider them in relation to the perspectives of others. "Dialogue may be external (between two different people) or internal (between an earlier and a later self)." (Holquist, p. 427) We also have internal dialogues when we retain and replay our own and someone else's voice. Sometimes, for example, when I am trying to work out an idea in my head, my daughter catches me: "Mom, you are talking to yourself again." Moreover, my thinking out loud is often aided by the hand gestures characteristic of lively debate among my Eastern European Jewish relatives. This book is designed to promote discussion and dialogue (internally and with others) because of the potential these hold for reconsidering, reshaping, or possibly just reframing and clarifying your educational ideas and practices.

STORY AND IDENTITY

 — for group

⌊It is not only through dialogue but also through story that we make sense of our own and others' lives.⌉ "In telling a fragment of his or her autobiography a speaker assigns parts and characters in the episodes described" (Davies & Harré, 1999, p. 3). In conversations, we may struggle with the positions others attempt to impose upon us. Afraid of being shot down by louder or more dominant voices, we may not say what we really think. In contrast, stories are a medium through which we may both select the positions we occupy and challenge the positions assigned to us by others. We can say what we think and feel, work out our ideas and concerns, and choose to share these if we wish. In the next chapter, Pansy expresses this idea in her vignette about identity entitled: "We have to write our own stories." She reflects on how important it is to create her own accounts of who she is and not to let others position or judge her ideas and actions.

Focusing on the idea of teachers as storytellers does not mean that teachers' work is the work of single authors. While these stories do express personal perspectives, the creative acts of imagination underpinning the stories are, like learning in general, not "one person act[s]" (Hanks, 1991, p. 15). Rather, these "acts" grow out of and are constructed in collaboration with a variety of people with whom they share their social and cultural worlds.

The vignettes in this collection, narrated in the teachers' own words, reveal a great deal about the complexities of identity construction. They are a rich source of information about struggles among the diverse discourses (e.g., traditional Ts'msyen and Haida knowledge systems, federal government and provincial education policies) that are involved in this process. The vignettes illustrate the varied and complex ways in which the narrators have been positioned – and have chosen to position themselves – in relation to an identification (First Nations), which might refer to legal definitions of the state, definitions based on race, language, culture, or some overlapping and contradictory combinations of these. In the vignette "I grew up in the city, I learned from my husband's parents", Marilyn creatively describes how she positions herself among the contradictory federal and Aboriginal authoritative discourses and creates her own sense of identity. She refers to policies imposed by the federal Indian Act that stress the importance of patrilineal ancestry, and the clan system of both her Haida father and Ts'msyen mother, in which matrilineal principles govern inheritance of clan membership.

The following chapter considers the complexities and struggles involved in identity construction. The vignettes illustrate the central importance of these ongoing struggles in the work and lives of these teachers and community members. Vignettes in Chapter 2, as well as in successive chapters, also illustrate the teachers' enthusiasm and creativity in crafting educational practices that distinctively include rich Ts'msyen and Haida resources, resources that are a growing part of the teachers' linguistic and cultural knowledge. Resources include knowledge of language, story, dance, and ecology, as well as daily practices of respect, generosity, and care for elders, learners, and the physical environment. These Ts'msyen and Haida practices are illustrative of the variety of Indigenous practices of teaching and learning further explored in Chapter 3.

CHAPTER 2:
IDENTITY AT THE CENTRE:
LINKING THE PAST AND THE FUTURE

We often hear our people say, "you have to know where you come from to know where you are going." In other words, our definition and self-determination as individuals and as nations involves calling on the past to define the future.

Anderson, 2000, p. 15.

In a discussion of native womanhood, First Nations scholar Kim Anderson cautions, however, that this does not mean "living in the past," but linking with and transforming it. In this perspective, the "past, present and future are understood to be inextricably connected" (2000, p. 16).

Cultural theorist Stuart Hall further specifies the idea that our histories do not determine our identities; rather, they are resources we can creatively draw upon in constructing our identities:

Identities are about using the resources of history, language, and culture in the process of becoming…:not "who we are" or "where we came from," so much as what we might become, how we have been represented and how we might represent ourselves. Identities relate to the invention of tradition as much as to tradition itself; not the so-called return to roots but a coming to terms with our routes. (1996, p. 4)

IDENTITY, LEARNING, AND TEACHING

Contemporary mainstream North American education emphasizes individuality as central to both learning and developing strong (independent) identities. Teachers frequently exhort us: "Do your own work" and "mind your own business." The identities we start building in school feed directly into our possibilities for vocational accomplishments as adults. Systems of testing and evaluation, which allow us entry to most careers, focus on our achievements as individual learners. Consequently, when we take up our vocational identities, we commonly assume that we have attained these identities based entirely on our own merits and individual performance.

In contrast, First Nations pedagogical theorist Linda Tuhuwai Smith (as cited in Battiste, Bell, & Findlay, 2002 and E. Hampton, 1995) as well as sociocultural theorists (Holland, Lachicotte, and Skinner, 1998; Wenger,1998) maintain that both learning and identity building are always social. These interconnected processes are continuously transacted in communal settings, whether these are the fishing boat, kitchen, classroom, or the community hall. Even being "alone" in nature can become a "social" enterprise. This is evident in Eber Hampton's description of the awareness he reached while fasting for a vision:[8]

> My identity expanded from my own skin outwards to family, friends, relatives, Indian people, other humans,...to finally reach the earth itself and everything that is.
>
> cited in Brant-Castellano, 2000, p. 19

Protocols in formal settings, especially where people from many nations are present, emphasize that social networks are integral to identity. Maori educator and scholar Linda Tuhuwai Smith puts it this way:

8 Ideas about spirituality and caring as identity practices will be explored further in Chapter 8, which focus on interactions with colleagues and students, and Chapter 9, which focuses on the development of new practices.

In our culture we begin by introducing ourselves by naming our geography, where we come from, then our ancestral lines, and then finally we name the people. In ancient times there was no need to know your name; that introduction was sufficient. But in modern times, I would say, "My name is Linda." It is important to begin in this manner as a way of identifying who we are, where we are from, and how we connect to everybody else.

as cited in Battiste et al., 2002, p. 169

By introducing themselves in the ways described by Hampton and Tuhuwai Smith, speakers acknowledge that their narratives are connected to history, community, and the environment. Pansy illustrates this same notion about identity when she begins her vignette in this chapter by identifying her membership in the Haida nation, and then tells us that her name in Haida is Oolongkuthway or "shining gold," a name given to her by her grandparents, her most important teachers in her early years.

Sociocultural theorist Etienne Wenger also emphasizes the social dimensions of learning and identity building, and specifies that learning "is in its essence, a fundamentally social phenomenon, reflecting our own deeply social nature as human beings capable of knowing." (1998, p. 3) "Moreover, learning is powerfully implicated in our identities, "changes who we are and creates personal histories of becoming in the context of our communities." (p. 5) Holland et al. further suggest that "identities are formed (learned) in the process of participating in activities." (1998, p. 57)

In many of the vignettes in this chapter, the teachers tell about ceremonial, subsistence, and family activities that are of ongoing importance to them in knowing who they are. Eva-Ann Hill, who grew up and now teaches in the small Gitga'at village of Txałgiu (Hartley Bay), writes about how her identification with Ts'msyen culture is grounded in subsistence activities that her husband's parents involve her in, such as gathering and preparing seaweed, and smoking fish. Marilyn Bryant also credits her husband's parents for including her in fishing, seaweed gathering, feasting, song, and dance in Lax Łgu'alaams (Port Simpson). She feels that these activities richly contribute to her sense of identity.

How do these insights into the social, activity-based nature of learning and identity contribute to our understandings of teachers' work? If teachers' identities are socially constructed, what implications does this have for their interactions with their students? Construction begins in childhood, as teachers learn from parents and grandparents, and continues over their life trajectories. What does the continuity of this process tell us about the learning and teaching processes that would support the identity work of the students in their classrooms?

Research on minority teachers in mainstream schools establishes that when these teachers bring their stories of identity to classrooms, they enrich and enhance students' learning (Beynon & Dossa, 2003; Thiessen et al. 1996; Ladson-Billings, 2001, 1994). The challenge for these teachers is that in their own schooling, including their university professional programs, they are commonly expected to suppress the cultural and linguistic facets of their identities that do not conform to the mainstream.

In contrast, the Prince Rupert First Nations Teacher Education Program centrally positioned First Nations cultural and linguistic identities as integral to the process of learning to become a teacher. A key objective in the teacher education program was to connect (and reconnect) with a larger community of Sm'algyax language speakers by means of a structured series of language courses that enrolled fluent speakers as well as novices.[9] So too does this book centrally focus on the teachers' perceptions of the linguistic and cultural facets of their identities, as well as how they see these facets figuring in their activities and identities as learners and teachers.

---

9 The fluent speakers were interested in the course because they wished to learn how to write Sm'algyax.

IDENTITY VIGNETTES

In preparing this book, we frequently discussed relationships between identity and teaching. Gregory Cajete from Santa Clara Pueblo in New Mexico focuses on the close links between education and identity.

> There is a shared body of understanding among many indigenous peoples that education is really about helping an individual find his or her face, which means finding out who you are, where you come from and your unique character.
>
> 2000, p. 183

In our conversations with one another, we asked "How did you find out about who you are, where you came from, and your unique character? Was this any part of your school experience? How does this knowledge figure into how you work with your students?"

This book presents the teachers' responses to these questions. In the vignettes in this chapter, teachers specify that their sense of themselves as Ts'msyen and Haida are connected to their kinship networks (through marriage as well as birth). First Nations languages, community subsistence, and ceremonial activities are also central in providing settings and resources for identity building. Anderson cautions, however, that individuals who do not have a "land-based" (2000, p. 27) experience may not easily be able to connect to large kinship networks, Aboriginal languages, or subsistence activities. Nevertheless, there are powerful aspects of identity that have no material markers. Respectful relations and self-respect are noted repeatedly by the teachers in this project as an integral dimension of how they understand identity, both their own and their students'. These deeply felt understandings – these "internally persuasive discourses" – echo Anderson's idea that "a sense of self and the individual is grounded within a sense of responsibility to community and relationships" (2000, p. 50).

Chaske (cited in Anderson, 2000) put it like this:

> How you live your life is also a ceremony. I have met many people who do not have the language, don't know any ceremonies, but they are the most traditional people I know. They are loyal, they are honest, they have integrity, they are caring, they know how to be respectful, they are all of those things that made our people who they are. All of those things that those ceremonies are meant to be.
>
> (p. 27)

Isabelle makes this point in her vignette entitled "Respect is key to my identity." She explains that while she didn't grow up in a village with extended family, her mother nevertheless emphasized the importance of respect in her relations with family. Ideas about caring and respect are further considered and specified by a variety of scholars, whose analyses of a range of Indigenous approaches to teaching and learning will be explored in Chapter 3.

Chapters 4 and 5 provide a chronology of the authoritative discourses sanctioned by the federal government and churches directing the education of Aboriginal youth in Canada. The conflicts and contradictions between official government and Indigenous approaches to education highlighted in these chapters are essential background for tracing the sources of the struggles that continue to surface in the teachers' daily efforts to nurture and strengthen their own and their students' identities.

Sometimes these struggles reflect contradictory expectations to honor, and enact their identities as Ts'msyen and Haida, as well as their identities as teaching professionals employed and governed by mainstream educational practices. Chapters 6 to 9 trace how teachers work their way through these struggles. Sociocultural theories (Holland et al., 1998) suggest that participation in a variety of settings (e.g. the community, the school, the professional association, and so on), each with its own discourses, contributes to our construction of identities that are correspondingly multifaceted. Hall puts it like this:

"Identities are constructed across different, often intersecting and antagonistic discourses" (1996, p. 4). This complexity both contributes to our struggles and provides resources and opportunities for creatively negotiating conflicts.

These ideas about struggle, creativity, multifaceted identities and diverse cultural worlds are explored more fully beginning in Chapter 6, which introduces the struggles that the narrators encountered in trying to find employment as teachers. This perspective is followed through in Chapter 7, which focuses on the world of the community, and Chapter 8, which looks into the world of the school and classroom.

SOME IDEAS ABOUT HOW TO USE THE VIGNETTES

The vignettes in this chapter, as well as those in Chapters 6 through 9, could stand by themselves as accounts of the challenges, successes, dead ends, hopes, conflicts, struggles, creativity, and collaboration that these teachers have experienced in their own education, in their work in school and community, and in the education of both their students and their own children. You may wish to simply read and reflect, think how you might have responded in the same circumstances, or even how you have already responded in similar circumstances. You might want to write down your own experiences, considering the responses you made and how you might respond differently if similar circumstances arose in the future.

You may also choose – building on your own reflections – to analyze the vignettes in relation respectively to ideas outlined in Chapter 1 about identity and change. How is your work connected to who you are? What are your aspirations and visions of the future for yourself and your students? How are ideas of liberatory pedagogy and agency important in the vignettes, and in your own work? What official discourses of schools have you had to struggle with in your own experiences as a student? What discourses do you struggle with in your work as a teacher? What steps can you take in your own learning and teaching to identify the barriers that interfere with your own and with your students' aspirations? How can you employ dialogue and story to support your efforts? How can you build on your identity, language, and experiences in family and community to bring change?

If you are reading the vignettes as part of a seminar or discussion group, together with the group facilitator you may wish to use the above questions, as well as similar ones at the end of each chapter, to stimulate dialogue. As you think about change, consider not only your own personal identity, but also how dialoguing and developing collaborative action with others can strengthen the possibilities for productive change in the locations in which you work. Creativity, identity, and change – like learning – are not one-person acts. Holland puts it well when she reminds us that identity combines the "intimate or personal world with the collective world of social relations"(1998, p. 5). Identities "do not come into being, take hold in lives or remain vibrant without considerable social work in and for the person. They happen in social practice" (1998, p. vii).

The vignettes in this chapter relate some of the practices that have helped teachers understand the complexity of their identities and begin charting rewarding educational journeys for themselves, their colleagues, and their students. Pansy, who lives far from Haida Gwaii, emphasizes the importance of writing to her. For Cam, it is teaching and living in the community where he grew up. These teachers talked to each other about what practices nourish them and help them retain and develop their energy and enthusiasm for working with the next generation.

Reading other teachers' stories can stimulate personal reflection and help you analyze the social and educational settings you work in. Respectful dialogue can lead to new insights, as well as encourage and support enthusiasm and creativity. As you read the vignettes, consider how you might collaborate with other educators and your communities in challenging the power relations that limit you. Think also about the resources of Indigenous pedagogies and your own identity, cultural, and linguistic resources that will enliven teaching and learning, not only for yourself and your Indigenous students, but for non-Indigenous students as well.

While going through the vignettes, keep these ideas about identity in mind: that it has to do with your roots but also with your routes; that it is about the traditions you inherit, but also about the ones you create as you struggle with the obstacles and constraints imposed in daily interactions with others and with the norms of the places where you live and work. The vignettes in this book illustrate a variety of ways in which one group of teachers are struggling with difficult circumstances, and how they are nevertheless creating vibrant educational opportunities for themselves and their students. Presenting their stories here is an invitation to you to become involved in the conversation and to carry it forward with your own colleagues. In sharing their experiences, these teachers are beckoning you into rich dialogues about learning, struggle, and change. These dialogues begin with stories of identity.

We have to write our own stories - Pansy

I am a Haida; I know who I am, I know my language and my culture. I was brought up by my grandparents. My first teachers were my grandparents, and my generation was able to learn a lot of our customs, traditions, and values, and that is the motivation of my personal self-esteem. Empowering myself to know who I was. The elders were our first teachers, and they are the ones who gave us encouragement to know our identity. My grandmother started a dance group when I was about 6 years old, and we went traveling all over. We went to Germany, Hawaii, all over Alaska with the Haida Eagle Dancers and she started teaching me to take over our dance group when I was about twelve years old. She was eighty-three when she died, and then I took over the group. I learned to use my crest to tell people who I was and where I belong. I didn't learn [about who I was] in the academic university. I couldn't learn that aspect of our traditions in that educational arena. It was all from home. So that is where my tradintional education came from.

I guess my strength is all the traditions that I live with. Most of my teachings have come from my grandmother and a few of the elders. Initially, I started writing about my grandmother through telling all the legends and the oral history of my family. There were the marriages, the arranged marriages, the beliefs of our own Haida traditions, songs, dances, names. Now it is opening up further and I'm including a lot of my own stories. It is changing. I find I have to write it from my own perspective. These stories have been passed down to me, so I need to write it in the third person. So now it's about me and my life; how I was brought up by my grandmother. I tell it as a person looking on, and I use my Haida name. It is Oolongkuthway, which means, "shining gold." I talk about Shining Gold. It's really hard to explain, but Haida people don't like to talk about themselves. In the third person, I can write about who I am without losing the integrity of our Haida customs. Our tradition is to let other people talk about how we are progressing. It is falling into place now, and the Education Master's program that I am taking has really helped me.

So many of our people are losing their identity. They don't know their clan, their crest, where they have come from. I think I have a lot to contribute to students, regardless of their age or grade, because I am genuinely concerned about our culture. I think I've got a really good rapport with the students. They see me as a native person and come up to me automatically. It's just easier for them to approach me because I am native. They don't have any second thoughts. I can understand their environment; where they came from. I can feel some of the struggles that their parents went through and after I get to know them, I can help out more. If there's a problem with anything: health, lack of food, I can easily talk to them. I guess there is automatic sensitivity to me. They are able to see who I am, that I am a teacher, and that I can help them.

For some of the students, even at the Grade 12 level, making that transition into the urban school is really frightening. To motivate them, you just build their self-esteem. I gave them a lot of different strategies of how to speak out: being proud of who they are, where they come from, and their identity. I help them in trying to build on their own unique character and incorporating the Sm'algyax and Haida languages when they are saying who they are. So that is where Sm'algyax and Haida come in, that First Nations component of the curriculum where they can learn the language, so they can be proud of their ancestry.

Through all the education I've had, I've learned to see a non-Native's point of view. A lot of the books that are written provide good historical facts, but we as First Nations people have to write our own stories. That's what I'd like to do. My Master's degree program is really helping me with this. I want to write a book about my grandmother; I want to teach, and perhaps make a difference as a teacher in mainstream education.

Who I am was just inbred right from the get go - Cam

Who I am was just inbred right from the get go. No ifs, ands, or buts. Just "this is what we do, this is when we do it, and this is how to do it." I can't even explain it any more than that. My dad should have spoken the language a lot more. My mom couldn't. She understands it all, but she couldn't. She didn't grow up with it. I don't know why my dad didn't talk to me in our language when I was younger. He did later on. It would have been so simple if he just talked to me like that when I was small.

I didn't want to leave Hartley Bay to go to Grade 11 in Prince Rupert. Grade 11 to me was hell. I hated it. I can't help but look at the Grade 5s I'm teaching now and think that in five years, those kids will be gone. They hit Grade 10, and they're gone. Kids in Hartley Bay have to grow up so much faster than anywhere else. I was ripped away from my mom and dad and I looked at it that way. Why wasn't there a Grade 11 and 12 there for me? I know there are a lot of kids who think they want to leave, but they don't.

I was in a pretty special group going through school. I really don't know why, but there were a whole bunch of us that graduated. Before that there had hardly been any. I can only think of maybe one grad, and then there was a span of about five to ten years with no graduates from Hartley Bay. Then there was our bunch, and now it seems there are none again. It's really sad.

If I had known in Grade 10 what I was in for, I would never have left. I was lucky enough to have a grandfather and grandmother in Rupert that I could stay with, and my mother's dad was there too before he died. He died in my Grade 11 year, and that made it even harder to get through the year. I had never cried before that year, and I remember the first week everything coming at me so strongly. In your first class no one says hello or goodbye. There's no one to say, "It's good to see you here." You don't fit in, you're surrounded by thirty other kids who couldn't care less about you. And then, as if that part isn't hard enough, you have no friends. You try to make them, but I just ended up sort of keeping to myself. I kept to my crew; that's what I called the kids that I came out of the village with. Toward the beginning of the first year they just started dropping. Six of us started, and there were only two left by June. Only two of us made it through Grade 11. Everyone started together again the next September, but the same thing happened. Only two of us graduated in the end.

I remember when my dad would come up to Rupert. He didn't come that often, but when he'd have meetings he'd come over and visit. We would go out for supper or whatever, and for about the first three quarters of the year, every time he'd leave I would just stand on the porch all by myself and just watch him go and then that's all I could think about. It was horrible, but I didn't turn to anybody else, and that made it tougher. I think I should be able to deal with stuff myself. I'm not the kind of person to pour out my troubles or lean on somebody else.

Respect is key to my identity - Isabelle

I learned my culture from my parents, my mom mostly. We were brought up in the city [of Prince Rupert], so we didn't know the village life, we didn't know the extended family, aunts and uncles. I hardly knew one set of grandparents. But it is what my mom taught us. She always taught us respect, and in certain situations you do this and that. It was just listening to your parents, is what I had. I wasn't lucky enough to be brought up in a village with a big extended family. I've done a lot of learning. All my learning now is through the elders I work with in the Sm'algyax language program. The respect I have for elders is key to my identity. They help you, and they respect you, and they are willing to share and exchange with you, and you can pass it on to your students.

There were very few First Nations kids in school when I was growing up. There are a lot of more First Nations kids in school now than when I was going through. When we teach the language [now] we are teaching culture and the meaning behind it, respect. What I am teaching and the teaching I received are very different. When I went to school, I just did the work and didn't remember the meaning. There was one exception. I remember one Grade 4 teacher who was First Nations, even though he didn't specifically teach First Nations [culture or language]. He wasn't from this area. I'll always remember him, because when he taught I remembered what he taught. I only remember him as a teacher I really liked and learned a lot from. What we are teaching [now] is meaningful. It is relevant; it is who we are. How we relate to the kids is so important. We are teaching what we want to pass on. It's a big difference. The more we stand out as First Nations teachers the better it is for the kids.

I grew up in the village . . .
I learned from my husband's parents - Eva-Ann

When I was going to school, because we are just a small community and we are all First Nations, I didn't pay attention to being First Nations. I didn't even identify the fact that I am First Nations. It was just school to me. But my parents, they don't speak the language, they understand it but they don't speak it, so the only language that I was learning was what was taught to us in school [English]. Whenever my family would be doing any sort of food gathering, the only thing that I ever remembered doing was either picking berries with my mother or going hunting with my father. I never learned how to harvest any of the other foods, or I was never really interested in trying to cut fish or anything like this. Whenever my parents were doing these activities, the kids in my family were sort of chased away to go play. Kids were not really there to help. So I didn't start any of those activities until I started going out with Cam. When I was with his family, that is what they did. They worked together and they gathered the food, they preserved it and that is when I started to become more aware of exactly what our culture was and what we had to do. So many of my experiences started with Cam and his grandparents and his parents. They were the ones who made me more aware of what it is to be First Nations and how to be First Nations. So that was when I became more culturally aware of who I am.

With my own family, my grandparents would use our language when they didn't want us children to know what they were talking about. But with Cam's they would explain. They would say it in Sm'algyax and then they would tell me what they are saying in Sm'algyax, and I would have to try to repeat and learn it. I have a hard time learning our language. I can tell you specific words . . . but understanding speeches I cannot do. I can get the gist of a speech, but I don't understand every single word they are saying.

We've been trying with our children right off the bat. We show them and try to teach them all about our language and the different things that are expected of them in our culture. With Rachel, for pretty much close to the first year Cam wouldn't speak anything but Sm'alyg̱ax to her and that was just wonderful. But he slacked off, and we keep bugging him about that.

I grew up in the city . . .
I learned from my husband's parents - Marilyn

I grew up in the city. I went to school in Prince Rupert too. My dad is Haida and my mom is Ts'msyen, and years ago my grandparents signed away their status. So my mother didn't have status, but gained Haida status when she married my dad. She was put on the Masset band list.[10] So I was brought up thinking I was Haida.

I don't remember experiencing all the First Nations language and culture that we now bring to the classroom. When I was going to school, I don't think that anyone saw my personality. I don't think anyone tried to get to know me and build on my strengths or anything. We were there to do our work until 3 o'clock, and then you were out. There is only one teacher that I remember. She was not First Nations, but she is the only teacher that I remember because she really tried to get to know her students and so that was really important. A lot of our kids are being told at home, "You are so bad. You are so rotten. I am sorry I ever had you." That kind of thing. Then they bring that to school, and we try to get them to see that they are good kids.

10 Through the Indian Act, the federal government imposed a structure of governance referred to as the "band council", consisting of elected representative (one for every 100 officially registered band members). The band list was the official government register of who was considered to legally be a community member. Membership was inherited through the paternal line, even in cultures like Haida and Ts'msyen, which are matrilineal. In communities traditionally governed by kinship groupings such as clans and hereditary chiefs, systems of traditional governance often continued alongside the new form. Often people who were the hereditary leaders were also elected to band councils.

Every kid is good, and so I think that having our background helps us to try to get the kids to achieve, to find their face and their heart.

When I moved to [Port] Simpson (my husband's community) I started seeing a lot of activities I had never done. I give my in-laws a lot of credit for showing me a lot of the traditional ways of things. My mother just wasn't shown these when she was growing up. So it is funny, because she grew up in Port Edward, and even though she worked in a cannery all her life, her family never did their own smoked fish. It just blew me away that when you go over to Simpson, everybody does their own smoked fish, but my parents were buying it when we were growing up. They were buying it from other people. So when my mom came over to visit [Port Simpson] we showed her how to smoke fish, and it was weird. It just felt weird, because in Port Simpson you just do your own or you don't get any.

I had never gone seaweed picking. When we were kids, we didn't do anything like the kids get to do in the village. So my in-laws were the ones who were really my teachers. They always harvested food, and they spoke Sm'algyax, and they knew all about feasting, you know, just everything. So that is who I learned a lot of it from; and then realized that I shouldn't be calling myself Haida, because my mother is not Haida. My mother is Ts'msyen, and in our tradition I follow my mother. My grandparents were around when I was growing up, but they were really, really hesitant to teach us anything about their background. My parents thought that the White way was the right way, and everything that they were doing was wrong. They wouldn't teach any of their kids the language. They both spoke Sm'algyax. They didn't want their kids knowing the language, because they couldn't use it in the White school and they wanted them educated in the White system. It was really sad. I mean it is very sad for my mother. Then my [paternal] grandmother, who taught the Haida language in the community, didn't teach her kids the Haida language. But my dad understands it. When my grandmother was alive, he could answer her when she spoke in Haida, but he wouldn't speak it.

So until I moved to Simpson and started having my own kids and worrying about if they are going to know who they are and where they are from, I was not thinking about these issues. I was lucky that my in-laws taught my kids who they are and where they are from, well, really taught my husband Sam and I. Sam is very knowledgeable, so our kids are lucky that they are getting this knowledge from him. Unfortunately, we can't pass on the Sm'algyax language to them because we haven't learned it either. That is the saddest thing that I see. We try to teach them everything else, but we just can't teach them the language.

Who I am and where I am from, it was just everybody that has been involved in my life who has helped to shape my life. Even the teachers who ignored me helped shape my life, because I knew and felt that that wasn't right. That isn't how a teacher should be. So it is just everyone that I've had contact with, from my former teachers to the teachers I had in university. Just everybody, everyone helps to shape who I am or how I think and how I see things. Mostly it is the kids in the school. They've had a huge impact on my life. My own kids too. I believe that I should never ask my kids to do anything that I wouldn't do. So if they are going to get up on the stage and do something, then I'm going to do it. I just found myself doing a lot of things that I never ever thought I would do. It is a lot of fun. Kids in my class have made comments like "God, you are like a kid."

SUGGESTED DISCUSSION QUESTIONS

In the vignettes in this chapter, narrators specify how a range of diverse people and locations were involved in how they understand their identities as Ts'msyen and Haida. In light of the experiences narrated in this chapter, consider:

1. What experiences have helped you to identify and support your linguistic and cultural ancestry? What experiences have been detrimental? What authoritative discourses of school or family have created obstacles? Which have been supportive? Have you had to struggle with contradictory discourses? What were these? How did you resolve them at that time? If they come up in future how do you think you will resolve them?

2. What were the cultural and linguistic backgrounds of your teachers? Did any of your teachers help you to discuss and explore issues of identity, or help you to learn more about language and culture?

3. If you wanted to learn about your ancestral language(s) and culture(s), what steps do you think you would take?

4. How might you go about helping your students to learn more about their own ancestral languages and cultures (or others)?

5. If you feel you have less knowledge than your students about their languages and cultures how might you, nevertheless, go about supporting their learning?

6. What examples do the narrators give of people learning languages and cultural practices from people other than their biological parents?

7. Are the cultures and languages of our biological parents the only ones to which we have authentic claims?

8.   What are the possibilities for authentically claiming identification with more than one language and a variety of cultural traditions?

9. What did you read (if anything) that seems to indicate that the narrators, or members of their families and communities, internalized mainstream discourses devaluing Indigenous languages and cultures? Have you had the experience of judging yourself by mainstream norms? Do you think there are times when it is okay and other times when you wish you wouldn't? How might you avoid doing this when you feel it isn't helpful?

10.   What ceremonies are important to you in your life? Is it possible to share any of these with your students?

CHAPTER 3:
LOOKING TO THE PAST:
SOURCES OF INDIGENOUS
EDUCATIONAL DISCOURSES

The vignettes in Chapter 2 specified a variety of links to community, family, and culture that are important to the teachers' identities. This chapter suggests how contemporary Indigenous ways of knowing (epistemology), and learning and teaching (pedagogy) are connected to practices that predate contact with Europeans. In examining the history of discourses that are implicated in Indigenous education, it is essential to start here. The works of Canadian and international scholars reviewed in this chapter provide rich insights into how these Indigenous discourses are implicated in teachers' identities and their work. Selected illustrations from the teachers' experiences introduce ideas that are elaborated in successive chapters.

A variety of educators (Battiste, 1995; Cajete, 2000; Calliou, 1995; Hampton, 2000; Medicine, 1987) helpfully specify the nuances and subtleties implicit in a variety of Indigenous North American traditions of knowing and learning. Brant-Castellano cautions against generalization, but does suggest the following useful overview regarding Canadian Aboriginal approaches: "Aboriginal knowledge is personal, oral, experiential, holistic, and conveyed in narrative or metaphorical language" (2000, p. 25).[11] Background on the personal, oral,

11 Additional research about 'traditional' styles of Indigenous discourse is intended to guide non-Indigenous educators' understandings of adjustments in their own speech, gestures, patterns of conversational turn taking etc. that will support students' participation in classroom settings (Scollon & Scollon, 1981; Stairs, 1993). Still other researchers usefully address the "participant structures," or ways teachers organize students and materials in order to bridge differences in culture, dialect, or power that obstruct learning (Kleinfeld, 1975; Phillips, 1983). In order to avoid stereotypes that impede effective pedagogy, this information needs to be considered in relation to the uniqueness of each cultural setting, as well as to individual learner differences within cultural communities.

experiential, holistic, and narrative/metaphorical aspects of knowledge provides a foundation for understanding the problems created by contemporary public schooling practices that contradict these approaches. Contradictions lead to some of the dilemmas presented in the teachers' vignettes. Analysis of the personal, oral, experiential, holistic and narrative reveal how a variety of cultural groups used language, story, technology and the arts to connect the generations to one another, as well as to the physical and spiritual worlds. They suggest how these approaches might be employed in contemporary settings to facilitate learning, and nourish the identities and communities disrupted by colonial and mainstream educational systems. (Armstrong, J, 2000; Battiste & Henderson, 2000; Hampton; 1995)

PERSONAL, ORAL, EXPERIENTIAL

The importance of language, narratives, and the elders in indigenous pedagogy accounts, in large part, for the personal, oral, and experiential dimensions of Canadian Aboriginal ways of knowing and learning.

LANGUAGE

Indigenous pedagogical theorists from Canada, the U.S., Australia, and New Zealand specify the powerful educational role of language. (Antone, Blair & Archibald, 2003; Battiste, 2000; Keeshig-Tobias, 2003) Prior to missionary efforts to write religious liturgies in Canadian Aboriginal languages, these languages were generally not written. Learning of all kinds required face-to-face communication that reinforced interpersonal, intergenerational social connections within family, clan, and community.[12]

---

12 One researched exception to this is Battiste's (1986) work on Mi'kmac, which makes the case that they displayed literacy in pictographs, petroglyphs, notched sticks, and wampums prior to the arrival of the French settlers.

The centrality of language in learning underscores that learning is a social enterprise. (Armstrong, 2000; Paulsen, 2003) The repository for much traditional knowledge is in traditional languages, and "as you learn the language you get a better knowledge of the culture" (Toulouse, 2003, p. 88). Consequently, much innovative work in Canadian Aboriginal education in the last thirty years has focused on recording and teaching these languages as fundamental to promoting the longevity and growth of Aboriginal cultures (Antone, Blair & Archibald, 2003; Kirkness, 1989, 1998; Young, 2003).[13] There are also important Indigenous language initiatives in the U.S. and New Zealand (Nee-Benham & Cooper, 2000; Smith, 2000).

In the Prince Rupert school district, fluent speakers, linguists, language resource teachers, and curriculum developers have been actively engaged for at least fifteen years in developing a sequenced program in Sm'algyax language. In the village schools, where all but a handful of students are Ts'msyen, the program starts in kindergarten. In the city, the program goes from Grades 5 to 12, and employs nine teachers. Sm'algyax is offered as an alternative to French; it provides another way for students to meet the provincial language requirement for second language instruction.[14] Some of the challenges and accomplishments of this program are explored more fully in Chapter 9. Although there are important initiatives in language and culture education in Haida Gwaii as well, these are beyond the scope of this book.

NARRATIVE

In the past, as in the present, it was not simply the language on its own, learned for its own sake, which was educationally

---

13   In March 2006, the British Columbia Ministry of Aboriginal Relations and Reconciliation announced a new one million dollar program to be directed toward language preservation and retention.
See: www2.news.gov.bc.ca/news_releases_2005-2009/2006ARR0012-000319.htm
14   Classes generally meet three times a week in forty minute blocks, and all of the teachers are provincially certified. Isabelle and Nadine, who contributed vignettes to this book, are staff members in this program.

critical. Languages conveyed their meanings in a rich array of narrative forms in a range of social, environmental, and spiritual contexts in which narratives were told, and in which language mediated interactions. (Anderson, 2004; Sterling, 2002) There is a variety of genres of narrative. These include oral history (e.g., family, clan histories), storytelling (teachings), oratory (speeches), and reportage (giving news and information). (Keeshig-Tobias, 2003) Although indicative of a wide variety of possibilities for oral transmission of knowledge rooted in Indigenous languages and genres, it is important not to use these as rigid categories.

For the Ts'msyen, the *adawx* are understood as the "true tellings, sacred history, or teaching narratives."[15] The telling of the *adawx*, often dramatized by expert singers and dancers wearing masks and regalia crafted by highly skilled artists and artisans, are also rich artistic expressions of social history and the arts (Kenny & Archibald, 2000) as well as of spiritual connections (Calliou, 1995; Curwen Doig, 2003) to the environment and ancestors (from *www.sd52.bc.ca/fnes/tsimshian/ct.html* Connecting Traditions: Explore Tsimshian Pre-Contact Life, retrieved November 7, 2007).

The curriculum developers and linguists in Prince Rupert created a variety of resources relating to social history, the arts, spirituality, and the environment. The six-book bilingual (Sm'algyax/English) series: *Suwilaay'msga Na Ga'niiyatgm / Teachings of Our Grandfathers* (Tsimshian Chiefs, 1992) are *adawx* told by elders, some first transcribed in 1920 by the Ts'msyen ethnologist William Beynon. They detail topics such as Ts'msyen trade and economy, important migrations, rituals of respect, and the sea otter hunt.[16] Other oral traditions include *adawx* that tell

15 The most important form of oral tradition for the Ts'msyen is the *adawx*. It is hard to give an accurate meaning for this word in English, but it can be translated to mean "true tellings", "sacred history", or "teaching narrative". These narratives contain the history of the Ts'msyen, and they explain the origins of the world from a Ts'msyen point of view. (www.sd52.bc.ca/fnes/tsimshian/tsim_index.html)

16 John Dunn, who also taught Sm'algyax language courses in the teacher education program, developed the orthography for these books.

about the origins of families, clans, and tribal groups. The Txamsm (Raven) stories, which are so numerous that they must be told in many sittings, tell how Txamsm brought order to the world; they also tell of his trickster characteristics of voraciousness, foolishness, and greed. Marilyn, Pansy, Isabelle, and Nadine are all skilled musicians and dancers who regularly participate in the community ceremonies and feasts where these stories are narrated. (retrieved November 7, 2007 from *www.sd52.bc.ca/fnes/tsimshian/ct.html* Connecting Traditions: Explore Tsimshian Pre-Contact Life.)

ELDERS

The central educational positions accorded to elders relates to their positions as narrators of these oral traditions. Among the Ts'msyen the sm'oogit, or chiefs (men) and sigidmhana'a (matriarchs) passed the oral record of historical events from one generation to the next (Tsimshian Chiefs, 1992).[17]

Elders were also knowledgeable about geography, subsistence and important social values. This knowledge positioned them as respected healers, religious practitioners, historians, genealogists, and "cultural professors"(Sterling, 2002). In a contemporary context, elders' knowledge of Aboriginal languages is a vital, yet ever-diminishing resource (Medicine, 1987). The Prince Rupert District Role Model program and the Ts'msyen curriculum framework and resource materials, provide opportunities for students to learn from the experiential knowledge of elders through participation in practices of fishing, food preparation, feasting, name giving ceremonies, carving, button blankets, dancing, drumming, and singing. Interactions with First Nations classroom teachers also support these experiences.

---

17 "Each chief who took part in one of these events told his (her) own eye-witness account in a feast for the approval of the other chiefs. He then taught this account to his heir until he had memorized it. After, when the heir became chief, he in turn taught it to the one who would succeed him. In this way history was 'written' in people's minds and passed on for hundreds of years" (Tsimshian Chiefs, 1992, Conflict at Gits'ilaasü).

Oral communication necessitates not only strong narrative skills, but strong listening skills as well. Nadine Leighton, one of the Sm'algyax language teachers who grew up in the Gitga'at village of Txalgiu (Hartley Bay) and now teaches Sm'algyax language to Prince Rupert secondary school students, works closely with elders to produce language-teaching materials. She reflects that learning from the elders requires listening. Her comment below also clarifies the importance that elders attribute to this face-to-face learning.

> Now that I'm no longer in school, the elders see me differently. I get a lot more information from them. Before, I was constantly asking them if I could record what they were saying for some course, and I think seeing me writing it down scared them. Now I don't ask. I just go and visit and I sit there until they're into a subject, and then I start asking questions.[18]

Focusing on knowledge that is personal and experiential also suggests an important educational role for narratives. Narratives make the circumstances in which knowledge was developed – or in which learning occurred – explicit. The vignettes in the present collection were stimulated by face-to-face communication. Narratives led to dialogues, and dialogues opened up opportunities for engaging with and struggling with each other's discourses. This engagement is critical to what Bakhtin (1981) referred to as our "ideological becoming": times when we begin to articulate the internally persuasive discourses that we find intensely meaningful. In Bakhtin's sense, the vignettes in this book chronicle these teachers' ideological becoming.

HOLISTIC

Aboriginal ways of knowing and learning emphasize that all areas of life and knowledge are interconnected. The Medicine Wheel is often used as a guide to analyzing problems

---

18 For Nadine's complete vignette, see "The Oral Tradition: Learning Through Listening" in Chapter 9.

and charting courses of action. Adapted from North American plains cultures, the wheel is divided into four sectors that symbolically represent the interconnections of the spiritual, emotional, physical, and cognitive (Calliou, 1995).

This idea of holistic relationships is relevant to the vignettes in this collection. In Chapter 2, teachers told us that their senses of their identities were based in physical activities like food gathering, which were rooted in the environment and subsistence technologies. These identity-affirming cultural practices also have strong connections to beliefs and practices about the importance of being respectful to one another and to the environment. These practices are not only important for First Nations. The notion of respect for the environment is central to tackling contemporary environmental issues regarding the need to balance technological, environmental, and resource concerns (Cajete, 1999; MacIvor, 1995; Snively,1995; Thompson, 2004).

Outlined below are some of the ways in which these holistic views of knowledge and learning are implicated in curriculum resource and program development, and the professional and personal lives of teachers, as well as the emotional lives of students.

RESOURCES AND ACTIVITIES

Language and culture programs connect students to "where they come from", and incorporate working with elders, community dance groups, or extended trips to fish camps for seaweed gathering, fishing, and food preserving. Bea Skog now teaches in Prince Rupert where she grew up, but her first few years of teaching were in village schools. She was very excited about the program she did in Lax Łgu'alaams (Port Simpson):

We're doing longhouses; all the four posts on each longhouse and the beams and so on. It's hands-on learning, and the students really look forward to doing it. We're trying to make it as authentic as possible, going down to the beach to collect materials.

Recreational activities such as all-Aboriginal basketball and baseball tournaments, in which students travel to communities away from school, also aim to connect students' physical and social selves to First Nations communities.

LIVES OF TEACHERS

Holistic approaches also provide a key perspective on the close connections between teachers' personal and professional worlds. The teachers continuously struggle with the desirability and practicalities of drawing boundaries and segmenting their lives into distinct personal and professional realms.

While committing themselves to enhancing the connections between the school and the community, teachers can also feel demoralized. In contrast to many mainstream teachers, they are not so easily able to create boundaries around their working lives. It is hard to leave their work at the classroom door. Cam put it this way:

I know the problems that go on in village life and I am able with deal with some of it, but a lot of it is just too hard. However, I am able to reflect on it and know who to ask, what to ask, because I have seen it before. I've seen it and I've known. There are lots of things that can bring you down - the whole gamut of village life: that people aren't happy, that there's not much employment. But you can't let that interfere with what you are doing with kids.[19]

The vignettes in Chapter 7 further illustrate the dilemma of balancing family and community relationships with teaching.

---

19 For Cam's complete vignette "Teaching where you grew up . . . serving your community" see Chapter 7.

LIVES OF STUDENTS

The idea that education is holistic refers not only to interconnections of various domains of knowledge. Holistic approaches also stress that learning must also support human growth and expression. As Cajete put it: "education should also help you to find your heart, which is that passionate sense of self that motivates you and moves you along in life (2000, p. 183).

Many of the vignettes in Chapter 8 recall teachers' intensely emotional experiences with students, and highlight the tremendous energy and commitment these teachers give to making the kinds of connections with students that will help them to express their "heart and their face" in the way that Cajete describes (2000, p. 183). With great compassion, they have attended to the complex emotional and intellectual webs of their students' lives.

Creating and supporting education that is personal, oral, experiential, and holistic involves struggles with the legacy of the colonial discourses of government and church that were intended to break up human connections, and to divorce young people from their cultures, elders, languages, communities, as well as their traditional notions of respect and spirituality. The teachers' struggles to reintegrate language, culture, and education are struggles that they are taking over from their elders. Their struggles with mainstream discourses of integration, provincial curriculum, and systems of assessment, accountability, testing, and graduation requirements are of more recent origin. The historical background to these struggles is outlined in Chapters 4 and 5.

Chapter 4:
Resisting Colonial Discourses of the Federal Government and Churches

People who confront an historical wall . . . may be able to tear it down, but they cannot ignore it. The wall is external to them, it precedes them, and they run into it, it is imposed on them . . . the historical act can never be abolished, as the very activities that are necessary to destroy it reveals.

(Varenne & McDermott, 1999, p. 180)

The metaphor of a wall aptly captures the colonial history of Aboriginal education in Canada. The federal government and a variety of churches, starting in eastern Canada in the early seventeenth century, powerfully employed schools to dominate, and eventually eliminate Aboriginal languages and cultures. Efforts to create different and better social futures must engage with these legacies. A succession of official federal discourses articulated in treaties, government acts, and statutes defined the school lives of Aboriginal young people. Teachers' commitment to the creative work of developing Sm'algyax language and Ts'msyen cultural programming grows from their resistance to these definitions.

In chronological order, this chapter outlines three main components of Canadian approaches to the education of Aboriginal peoples. A broad overview of Canadian federal policies regarding responsibilities for Aboriginal education dating to the 1800s is followed by a summary of the government authorized residential school system operated by a variety of religious denominations. Subsequent government efforts to integrate First Nations into mainstream provincial schools are then outlined. For each of these three components, details of how these national initiatives played out locally in the Ts'msyen territories are specified.

CANADIAN FEDERAL POLICIES

James Youngblood Henderson's analysis of the Crown's treaties with Aboriginal peoples in Canada clearly establishes the early origins of the local control discourse articulated in 1972 by the National Indian Brotherhood in the Indian Control of Indian Education policy paper. "The First Nations treaties with the imperial Crown created an educational right in the Aboriginal families and a corresponding duty or obligation on the Crown to finance educational facilities and opportunities (Henderson, 1995, p. 245).

Furthermore, "The First Nations never delegated to the Crown any role in educating their people . . . Aboriginal choice continues as a constitutional obligation, which has never been extinguished although it has been regulated by different governments (Henderson, 1995, p. 247).

Canadian federal legislation and treaties established with the Crown specified how schools were to be financed, and where they would be conducted (initially on reserves and then in residential schools). An overview of key events, beginning with Canadian Confederation in 1867, followed by a succession of revised Indian Acts (1876, 1927, 1951) is provided in Appendix 3.

The federal acts (1876, 1894, 1920) and the subsequent Indian Acts of 1927 and 1951 strengthened government authority over schools far beyond any earlier power delegated (or abrogated) by Aboriginal peoples. Federal authority included provision of funding, responsibility for staff selection and employment, and designation of courses of study. In fact, the federal government directed funding to the variety of religious denominations that had already developed the infrastructures for schools. The specificities of how this was done varied from province to province, and regionally within provinces.

NORTH COASTAL REGION

Susan Neylan's *The Heavens are Changing: Nineteenth Century Protestant Missions and Tsimshian Christianity* (2003) provides a detailed overview of missionary activity in north coastal British Columbia. She documents the strong presence of three Protestant denominations: Anglican, Methodist, and Salvation Army. All used Sm'algyax orally, and in a written form, to support their evangelical work.

> For the Protestant denominations active in the North Pacific Coast area, there does not appear to have been an immediate proscription against the use of indigenous languages in schools or in church services. The same was not true for other areas of the Coast or for different denominations. (p. 145)

In Lax Łgu'alaams (Port Simpson), the missionary William Duncan opened the first school in the 1850s. School was also central to the utopian Methodist community he established in Maxłaxaała (Metlakatla) in 1862.[20] The missionary Thomas Crosby, who succeeded Duncan at Port Simpson, simultaneously devalued First Nations spirituality and designated the western institution of school as the site for its subversion when he wrote that "our way to a heathen tribe was often through the school" (Bolt, 1992, p. 63).

However, children did not consistently attend (day) school, because family subsistence activities of fishing, hunting, and trapping entailed seasonal migrations. In order to improve attendance, Crosby's wife Emma established a girls' boarding home in Port Simpson (1879) where students could lodge while their parents were away from the villages. Retrospectively, Thomas Crosby wrote:

---

20 All Ts'msyen community names are shown in Sm'algyax with common names in parentheses (Campbell, 2005, p. 218).

The missionary finds among a people that are so constantly moving about that if he is to expect real, good work it must be done by gathering a number of the children together in Home or Boarding school or Industrial Institution where they can be kept constantly and regularly at school and away from the evil influences of heathen life.

(Crosby, 1914, p. 84; as cited in Archibald, 1996, p. 293)

Discipline was rigid, and the objective was to train girls in cooking, sewing, hygiene, mothering, and serving. In 1890, a boys' school was added (Bolt, 1992, p. 62). Parents who wanted their children to have an education sometimes had to sign away their rights to these children for a three-year period (Campbell, 2005, p. 129).[21] In 1898, the missionary Elizabeth Shaw wrote to the Women's Missionary Society of her shock at the practices in these schools, including flogging (Campbell, 2005, p. 127).

In spite of these oppressive conditions, historical documents for Canada in general, and the north coast of British Columbia in particular, make clear that when Aboriginal educators work for local control of their current education, they are building on a substantial history of First Nations involvement in education and Christian mission work. The story of the north coast village of Maxłaxaała (Metlakatla), in which Methodist Christianity was practiced with considerable interweaving of Indigenous spirituality and social practices, is well documented (Bolt, 1992; Duff, 1964; Neylan, 2003). Moreover, during this period there were a number of ordained missionaries whose mothers were Ts'msyen[22] and whose fathers were of Anglo-celtic ancestry.

---

21 Campbell illustrates missionary powers in the following quote from an authorization form parents had to sign if they wanted their children to attend school: "I . . . hereby surrender to Thomas Crosby of Fort Simpson, missionary of the Methodist church, my daughter to keep, clothe, and teach for three years. And I do hereby give the said Thomas Crosby full control to have full power, control and authority, to bind out my daughter for service, for trade or for adoption" (2005, p. 129).
22 In Ts'msyen tradition membership in clans is in the mother's line of inheritance.

Biographical details indicate that these missionaries spoke English and Ts'msyen, and traveled widely along the coast. In addition, there were numerous Ts'msyen lay mission or church workers who taught in the village schools run by the churches.[23]

RESIDENTIAL SCHOOLS

The 1894, Act of Parliament officially authorized residential (or boarding) schools as a replacement for village-based schooling. Teachers in these boarding schools (like their predecessors in the village schools) were commonly members of religious orders trained in eastern Canada. Curriculum was Christian religion, basic English, computation, and a variety of vocational programs: e.g., farming, stock-raising, and "housewifery" (cooking, cleaning, and sewing), which provided for the material needs of the institution (Archibald, 1996). The dual aim of these institutions was annihilating Aboriginal cultures and languages, and converting young people to Christianity.

To varying degrees, in part associated with how far from home children needed to travel, and how seldom they were able to visit home, a variety of institutional practices silenced the voices of parents, and grandparents. Their voices were largely excluded from the conversations vital to the education and identity processes of their children (Haig-Brown, 1998; Sterling, 1992). Unlike those attending the Crosby's Girls' and Boys' school in Port Simpson, most students traveled considerable distances to attend school. These institutions were intended, as Crosby specified, to Christianize young people and to strip them of their languages, cultures, and identities.

23 In 1884, within the Methodist church, there was a total of sixty-seven Native mission or church workers: thirteen local preachers, ten local exhorters, eighteen class leaders and twenty-six stewards. (B.C. Methodist Conference minutes, Annual Port Simpson District Meeting, 1884, cited in Neylan, 2003, 303). Ts'msyen people were similarly active in the Salvation Army and the Church Missionary Society, but figures were not recorded.

Concurrently (and by the end of the nineteenth century) nearly 50% of the children attending these schools died, mainly from tuberculosis (Kirkness & Bowman, 1992). Documentation is growing of the physical and mental brutality involved in efforts to annihilate languages and cultures. Supreme Court decisions in the last ten years acknowledge church culpability and some individuals who were sexually abused in these institutions have received a degree of financial restitution (Department of Justice, Canada, 2005). Most recently, the federal government has allocated more than twenty billion dollars to address compensation, and approximately 80 000 Indian residential school students were invited to attend the hearings at various locations across Canada in the fall of 2006 (Mulgrew, 2006).[24] Unjustly, this compensation does not include Métis (Clarke, J., 2006).

In the context of this historical framework, the authoritative discourses of government exercised through the churches predominated. Church officials well understood the minimum requirements for maintaining Aboriginal languages, and acted to dismantle these essentials. For example, children in residential schools were prohibited from speaking their ancestral languages. If they were caught using these languages, they were punished. Siblings and children who spoke the same languages were often sent to different schools. This strategy separated them from others to whom they could speak their language. It also deprived them of other social and emotional supports to their linguistic and cultural identities. In many schools, the only common language was English. Nevertheless, in spite of the efforts to eliminate the languages, small numbers of fluent speakers have endured.

Recent analyses that build on personal narratives of a variety of First Nations peoples chronicle successful individual and collective struggles against oppressive practices of government

---

24 This sum was used for travel and legal fees as well as compensation.

and state (Haig-Brown; Secwepemc Cultural Education Society, 2000, Sterling, 1992).[25] Specific instances when individual nuns and priests were supportive and caring, and individual students exercised their resistance to oppressive practices are documented as well (Glavin, 2002; Lomaiwaima, 1994). For instance the Secwepemc [Shuswap] children at Kamloops Indian residential school found brief times and spaces away from supervision for using their language (Haig-Brown). One woman recounts going over words and phrases in her own mind before she fell asleep every night. One girl made up an "Indian" dance to entertain the nuns. She accompanied it with a song (in Secwepemc) that referred to one of the sisters as the "dirty behind nun" (Haig-Brown, p. 92). Summer visits home afforded a few months of language immersion, as well as encouragement from parents and grandparents that helped many youngsters to maintain their language (Sterling, 1992).

Moreover, there are examples in some narrative accounts of former students from St. Mary's School in Mission, B.C. (e.g., Glavin, 2002) of students making it clear that occurrences of abuse do not fit a simple pattern; the worst abuses were associated with specific priests and nuns who were a minority. Martina Pierre attended from 1950 to 1964. A member of the Lil'wat Nation, she is a fluent speaker of her language. As a B.C. certified teacher, she has taught at the band-controlled school in Mt. Currie, B.C. for the past twenty-five years. Martina said:

> I felt like a lost person, not worthy of the White man's God . . . it seems that we were always doing wrong and being sinful. I was sure in line for the strap every night before bedtime. It seems there was a continuous list of bad behaviours discovered everyday.
>
> (Glavin, 2002, p. 56)

---

25 Neylan notes a similar pattern in the missions in the North Coast region of B.C. In her study of native Christians, native mission workers and native missionaries she focuses centrally on the ways "Northwest Coast peoples actively took part in missions, shaped and defined the processes of their own Christianization, yet they never could entirely direct or control them" (2003, p. 5).

On the other hand, Bill Williams, chief of the Chehalis band (Stölo First Nation) for over twenty years, recounts that when he attended in the late 1940s and early 1950s, he never had any negative experiences. Glavin notes that some four fifths of Aboriginal leadership in the region surrounding St. Mary's are graduates of this school.

In a similar vein, some of the male graduates of Kamloops recounted that in the late 1940s with the arrival of a new principal, a few boys (five of 300) considered to be academically gifted were selected to participate in small group seminar discussions with priests on issues of philosophy. One graduate said about this priest: "he respected our ideas, no matter how small they were", and told them about possibilities for attending university, "where your mind can keep on going" (Haig-Brown, p. 73).

Lomawaima (1994), documenting the Chilocco school in Oklahoma, also suggests that personal narratives of school graduates give a more nuanced and complex picture of individual students' experiences than is evident in official documentary data. In particular, during the depression of the 1930s, the school was a safe haven where there was adequate food and clothing, as well as preparation for a trade. The official records document a school run along military rather than religious protocols, with selected superintendents perceived as concerned about the students' best interests. For some families, the school was a valued alma mater that had served several generations well. Historian Jean Barman aptly sums up the contradictions between official oppression and individual good will in Canada:

> While teachers and administrators of good will were able to ameliorate the worst aspects of the system for their pupils, all of the individual good will in the world could not have rescued a system that was fundamentally flawed.
>
> (1995, p. 57)

NORTH COASTAL REGION

Resistance on the north coast to federal government intentions to place students in residential schools outside of Ts'msyen territory is illustrated in a number of documents.[26] Taken together, these suggest that with the exception of the boarding homes for local students described above, larger distantly located residential schools were not a prominent feature of education for north coast youth until the 1950s.

A letter written in February 1897 from the Gitxaała (Kitkatla) community to the Minister of Education for Indian Affairs illustrates that there was explicit opposition to taking children from their homes. The letter requests a school similar to the one at Maxłaxaała (Metlakatla), but smaller, so that the children would not have to leave the village of about 250 residents. Also in the village of Gitxaała (Kitkatla), the register of attendance filed by the teacher with the Government of Canada from 1914-1916 records thirty-nine students between the ages of nine and fifteen in attendance (Horton, Trerise, Gale, & Carboni, 1994). In March 1897, the Chiefs of the Indian Council of Lax Łgu'alaams (Port Simpson) requested that the Department of Indian Affairs contribute to the running of the village school built by the Crosbys and Methodists twenty years earlier.[27]

Accounts of the village of Hartley Bay include a reference to the annual report of the Missionary Society (1890-91). This report stated that the village was "in great need of a native teacher in the winter session" (as cited in Campbell, 1984, p. 14). Funding by the Department of Indian Affairs did not begin until 1905.

---

26 There is no comprehensive account of this period comparable to Neylan's work on the earlier period. Gaps (from approximately 1910 to the 1950s) in the documentary record reviewed here reflect difficulties in accessing records housed in Ottawa from British Columbia. Nevertheless, documentation available locally, through the Provincial Archives of British Columbia, give some idea of the sequence of educational arrangements and the discourses of both First Nations and church articulated during this period.

27 Correspondence from the Public Archives of Canada, Indian Affairs (RG 10 Volume 6458, file 886-1 part 1, documents 154334, 154064).

Fifteen children were enrolled (village population was in the 90s). The teacher was Anglo; he was also the pastor, and taught the children in his house. He left in 1907, and for the next three years there were two replacements, as well as periods with no teacher. Visiting in 1909, the school inspector said "the children are very intelligent and do well in their studies." He also reported that the parents took an interest in their children's education, and were upset at the continual change of teachers. In 1910, Reverend Peter Kelly was posted to the mission and built a schoolhouse costing $1350 (Campbell, 1984, p. 21).

While it wasn't until 1920 that the federal governor-in-council was given authority to establish day schools on reserves (Henderson, 1995), it appears that coastal Ts'msyen villages had a continuous history of schools in the villages.[28] Archival correspondence indicates that the formal discourse of local control articulated in 1972 had its roots many decades earlier.

British Columbia archival materials dating from the late 1950s document that students from the north coast went to distant residential schools in Edmonton, Alberta (Catholic), Port Alberni and Sardis (Methodist), and Alert Bay (Anglican). They were only able to return home in the summer. Among the teachers contributing to the present book, there were accounts of older siblings, parents, or grandparents who were students in these schools. This negatively impacted their own opportunities for hearing and learning Sm'algyax and Haida. Recall Marilyn's comments in Chapter 3 about how her parents were reluctant to use their languages, because they were concerned it would have negative impacts on her own English language education. Questions about how to appropriately address this history of residential school experiences with their students also figure in the teachers' classroom work (see vignettes in Chapter 9).

---

28 It may be that it was not until the 1920s or after that the federal government took on direct financial and administrative responsibility, i.e., employed lay teachers, but documentation of when this change occurred was not available.

DISCOURSES OF INTEGRATION:
THE DEPARTMENT OF INDIAN AFFAIRS,
THE PROVINCES, AND THE SCHOOLS

In the years after the Second World War, the federal government ceased contracting with churches, and initiated legal agreements with provincial governments for the education of Aboriginal children. This policy change was referred to in official government discourse as "integration," a term which filtered down into educational circles.

> By 1951 the federal government had replaced the missionaries' authority with a perceived unlimited power to demand integrated education . . . The minister of Indian Affairs was authorized to enter into agreements with provincial and territorial governments for Indian education. (Henderson, 1995, p. 253)

The policy of integration was in actuality designed to assimilate Aboriginal children, and was introduced and continued with little or no consultation with Aboriginal parents or their children. First Nations educator Verna Kirkness makes it clear that "This program has not been one of true integration where the different cultures are recognized; rather, it has been a program of assimilation where First Nations students are (expected to be) absorbed into the dominant society" (Kirkness & Bowman, 1992, p. 12).

In fact, the "absorption" required very little of the mainstream. First Nations children and their parents were expected to do all the work of cultural and linguistic change. In sociological discourse, "integration" means that two sets of people or systems come together, and each retains unique linguistic and cultural practices. The "integration" of Aboriginal students was what sociologists refer to as "assimilation," the suppression and replacement of one language and culture by those of the dominating society. The official discourse of integration masked daily assimilative practices.

Central to the logic of the integration discourse was the idea that Aboriginal people were caught between two cultures. Either total assimilation into mainstream culture or attempts to live entirely according to traditional patterns were identified as the only alternatives. The latter was seen as a lost possibility. Hence integration into public schools needed to be pursued for the presumed welfare of Aboriginal children (Hawthorn, Tremblay, & Ryan, 1967).

Research (Stairs, 1993; Wyatt, 1978/79) based on observations and first-hand accounts of Aboriginal teachers in their classrooms illustrate that the experience of being caught between two cultures was not inevitable. At least within the world of the classroom, many Aboriginal teachers were able to make connections between two cultures by bringing community cultural practices into mainstream curriculum. They were disrupting and "talking back" to the authoritative discourses imposed on them by government policies that outlined either segregation or assimilation as the only available choices. The collection of vignettes in this volume contributes to a growing body of research on how Indigenous teachers in Canada, the U.S., Australia, and New Zealand are innovatively bringing Indigenous pedagogical practices into mainstream educational settings (Nee-Benham & Cooper, 2000). These approaches illustrate how teachers can avoid either/or choices, and creatively synthesize aspects of two pedagogical systems.[29]

In the early 1950s, fewer than 8.5% of Aboriginal students attended public schools. By 1972, the figure was over 60%. In many cases, the residential schools continued to serve as dormitories for students attending provincial public institutions.

---

29 Similar educational response to this proposed dichotomy was that bicultural educational programs could prepare students and their teachers to "walk in two worlds." Henze and Vanette (1993) examine this argument in the context of Yupik Alaskan programs and demonstrate that walking in two worlds is an unrealistic vision premised on the inaccurate notion that Indigenous cultures remain unchanged and that Indigenous people only have two choices. Building educational programs from this perspective, they argue, "masks the complexity of choices and reduces options" (p. 116).

Presently, Aboriginal students predominantly attend provincial schools, but many (especially secondary school students from rural areas) must still live away from their home communities, generally boarding with families in towns where schools are located. Some students, especially those in elementary grades, have been able to attend band-controlled schools, initiated at varying times since the 1970s.

NORTH COASTAL REGION

While the possibility of supposed integration into provincial schools began in 1951, it appears that in the north coastal region this did not happen immediately. The long-standing operation of village-based schools (first under church jurisdiction and then under federal jurisdiction) meant that "integration" primarily affected students after the elementary grades, usually beginning in Grades 8 or 9. Correspondence from the Northcoast Regional Indian Superintendent to the Vancouver Regional Office indicates that in response to parental objections to sending children to residential schools in Alert Bay, Lytton, Port Alberni, or Edmonton, hostels or home boarding programs (rather than residential schools) should be initiated in Terrace and Prince Rupert.[30]

Students from Lax Łgu'alaams (Port Simpson) were attending provincial secondary school in Prince Rupert in 1960 when the First Nations Liberal M.P. from Skeena, Frank Howard, initiated a request to Department of Indian Affairs (DIA) to allow them to live in Lax Łgu'alaams while attending school in Prince Rupert (rather than having to live in hostels or boarding homes). Accomplishing this required building an all-season road twenty-five miles overland to connect the village to the city of Prince Rupert. The existing means were lengthy ferry journeys or costly floatplanes.

---

30 This argument was also fuelled by the expression of concern from Edmonton that they no longer had spaces for children from British Columbia. (January 6, 1959). Memo from Education Division, Regional Office, Vancouver to Indian Affairs Branch Canada.)

However, the cost of building a road was calculated to be more expensive than paying for the boarding home program.[31] In 1961, the Indian superintendent for the Skeena River Agency recommended to the Indian commissioner for B.C., without success, that a hostel for 150 students be constructed in Prince Rupert to accommodate students Grade 6 to 12.[32]

Throughout the 1960s, DIA correspondence also indicates a range of educational issues, including the formation of village school committees, need for indoor play space, and additional classroom space to accommodate Grade 9 and 10 students so they would not have to leave the communities to attend secondary school in Prince Rupert. The Skeena Region DIA superintendent initiated the idea of forming a community school committee in Port Simpson. He wanted this committee established more quickly than it was, and was not comfortable with what appeared to be the appointment (rather than the election) by the band council of committee members.[33]

Subsequent letters and minutes indicate that the business of the committee largely regarded daily concerns such as finding appropriate indoor play spaces during inclement weather and organizing the Halloween party. Committee minutes from the mid-1960s however, identify the following substantial topics that were of considerable significance for students' education: the need for counseling Grade 8 youth before they go off to residential school and the need for four more classrooms (as opposed to the two that DIA was proposing). Also salient was the proposal by the committee to incorporate the kindergarten into the school with attendant need for space and desire to employ the incumbent teacher under a DIA contract.[34]

---

31 At present, the road link is being improved. An all-season road from Lax Ḻgu'alaams is being extended to a ferry connection that links to Prince Rupert in a relatively short voyage.

32 This is documented in correspondence between the band, the school district, and DIA that also indicates considerable disagreement over whether road construction costs would be a federal or a provincial responsibility. Public Archives of Canada. Indian Affairs (RG 10, Volume 8763, File 984/25-1S).

33 He was also concerned that there were no women on the committee.

As the villages were working to make it possible for their children to stay at home longer, DIA began to transfer responsibility for these students to provincial jurisdiction. In 1970, the DIA director of the Education Branch, Ottawa, wrote to the regional DIA director for B.C. and the Yukon indicating that, nationally, 60% of "Indian" students were enrolled in non-federal schools, and he was interested in having this go to 100%.[35] The intent to move in this direction was coincident with the White Paper policy (1969), a new federal policy that sought to transfer federal responsibility for "Indian" education to the provinces (Battiste, 1995, p. viii).

DISCOURSES OF ASSIMILATION AND AUTONOMY: THE ONGOING STRUGGLE FOR CONTROL

The White Paper policy proposed that provincial schools would inevitably absorb all [Indian] students. Objections to this policy were articulated in the Red Paper policy that led to the National Indian Brotherhood's 1972 Indian Control of Indian Education. This policy document clearly and forcefully articulated that the federal government should begin devolving its powers to First Nations communities. Hence, First Nations parents and teachers would be centrally positioned to rebuild the social, linguistic, and cultural structures of their communities, previously disrupted by colonial and post-colonial governments and churches. The paper specified the following three interlocking objectives necessary to achieve this goal: to prepare First Nations teachers, to develop curriculum reflective of First Nations cultures and languages, and to involve parents and community in formulating school objectives, policies, and programs.

The reform discourses articulated in this policy paper were taken up in varied ways in different communities across Canada.

34 Up to this point, the kindergarten was held in the church, and the band education committee was arguing that it was important to the longevity and continuity of the program to incorporate it as a regular offering in the school.

35 Personal communication from J.G. McGilp, director of the Education Branch to F.A. Clark, regional director, B.C. & Yukon Region, Jan 22, 1970 (Document 901/1-2-2-9E).

A number of communities considered that it was in their best interests to set up their own band controlled, community/ village-based schools funded directly by the federal government. In some instances, this entailed taking over responsibility for day schools on the reserves that had previously been administered by the Department of Indian Affairs and staffed either by clergy or civil service employees.

Demographic factors, proximity to regional urban centers, and diversity of Aboriginal languages and dialects were some of the local characteristics implicated in the models of schooling and teacher education pursued by different communities (Beynon, 1985,1991; Wyatt, 1978/9). A number of communities that chose to establish band-controlled schools used former federal day school buildings (Beynon, 1985,1991). In many parts of Canada, federal funds were transferred to provincial ministries of education for subsequent disbursement to local school districts under an arrangement referred to in British Columbia as the Master Tuition Agreement. This two-party agreement between DIA and the Province of British Columbia excluded the key third party: the First Nations communities. This exclusion has long been an impediment to First Nations communities exercising any influence over how the federal funds transferred to the province would be spent at the local district level.

North coastal region

Soon after 1973, First Nations in the Prince Rupert district, (which includes the city of Prince Rupert, as well as the village schools) decided to transfer educational services to the provincial school district rather than to develop band-controlled schools. The initial negotiations in the 1970s regarding what was sometimes referred to in official documentation as the "amalgamation," and sometimes the "take-over," are outlined in the next chapter.

CHAPTER 5:
ON THE THRESHOLD OF CHANGE: STRUGGLES BETWEEN DISCOURSES OF INDIGENOUS EDUCATIONAL REFORM AND MAINSTREAM DISCOURSES

How did the Ts'msyen and Haida First Nations position themselves and insert their discourses of change into the nation-wide struggles with federal and provincial policies? In the Prince Rupert region, there was a long history of involvement of Ts'msyen villages in education. This chapter reviews available school distict archival materials that document advocacy at the village level, and examines the rationale to become affiliated with the provincial district rather than setting up band-controlled schools. New administrative developments between the provincial Ministry of Education the Prince Rupert District also opened up opportunities for Ts'msyen advocacy.

AFFILIATING WITH THE DISTRICT

In 1973, shortly after the Indian Control of Indian Education position paper affirmed new educational possibilities, the Ts'msyen communities (with the Department of Indian Affairs brokering the arrangement) began to negotiate a relationship with Prince Rupert School Board. There is scant print documentation of the band education authorities' decisions to have the Department of Indian Affairs direct educational funds to Prince Rupert district provincial schools, rather than trying to establish their own band-controlled schools. However, interviews with Ts'msyen government officers and former school officials indicate that a few key and trusted administrators working for DIA recommended that school district services were more diverse, specialized, and better funded than what DIA customarily provided.[36]

36 Special thanks respectively to Robert Sankey and Jack Lowe.

Moreover, teachers employed by a public district would be required to have a higher standard of training, would have resources for supplies, and books and materials would be more plentiful.

Also during this post-1973 period, several strategically positioned school district officials were considered supportive of Ts'msyen educational concerns, and willing to engage in dialogue regarding the kinds of services and programs that would be available, including programming responsive to the unique histories and linguistic resources of Ts'msyen children. The path to affiliation required negotiation regarding the construction of new facilities, addition of Grades 8 to 12 in the village schools, travel costs for specialists, and school board meetings, as well as language and culture programs and curriculum development. The development of sophisticated First Nations advocacy and a growing cadre of First Nations education professionals were instrumental in shaping this process.

NEW BUILDINGS NEEDED

The lengthy seven-year amalgamation/take-over process (1972-1979) was finalized in conjunction with the completion of new village school facilities.[37] Requests to DIA for new buildings were initiated in February 1974 and by May 1979 all three villages - Txałgiu (Hartley Bay), Lax Łgu'alaams (Port Simpson) and Gitxaała (Kitkatla) - had new buildings. The district expressed great concern that they would be faced with substantial construction and maintenance costs. It seems likely that the district was waiting for the construction to be completed before bringing the village schools officially into the district administration. It is also clear that the band councils were not prepared to proceed with the transfer until they were certain that school facilities met their needs.

---

37 Appendix IV contains entries from School District meeting minutes, and DIA correspondence and documents that record this process.

KEEPING THE KIDS AT HOME

School board minutes and correspondence indicate that each of the three villages wanted to have a sufficient number of classrooms to accommodate Grade 10 students, and that they were also working toward the eventual accommodation of Grades 11 and 12.[38] A 1974 Gitga'at Band Council resolution requesting that Grade 9/10 be taught in Hartley Bay (requiring a teacher salary, and outfitting a classroom and a house for the teacher) included a detailed rationale that articulates the importance of local autonomy.

> The Hartley Bay Band Council and School Committee feel their young people would greatly benefit from the opportunity to remain at Hartley Bay and attend high school from their own homes. Past performance indicates that students have been happy and have succeeded academically in their home environment. Upon leaving home to be boarded out, they have had serious social and academic problems leading to their dropping out. It is felt that the students will feel more secure and be more successful if allowed to remain at home and attend high school, thus developing a strong personal and cultural identity. (February 14, 1974)[39]

Recently, Hartley Bay has prevailed, and students are now able to complete Grade 12 in their village.

---

38 In 2002, the Lax Łgu'alaams (Port Simpson) band education committee decided to withdraw from this arrangement, and to set up a band-controlled school (The Coast Tsimshian Academy) offering Grade 12 completion. In March 2007, it was honored by the BC Ministry of Education as one of eight outstanding schools in the province. The development of the secondary program is facilitated by the growth of online offerings of a number of secondary school courses by the B.C. Ministry of Education.
39 BCR #71, Document 98413-2-10. Personal correspondence from E. Hill, principal, Hartley Bay School.

TRAVEL AND PERSONNEL

School board minutes (September 2, 1975) also refer to the travel costs associated with providing services to the villages (special education and counseling in particular, where each school did not have a resident specialist). Costs of bringing village representatives to board meetings was also a concern articulated by the board. Villages were invited to send representatives to these, but they could not vote, and the district would not pay their travel costs. Presumably, the DIA was expected to do so. On the other hand, when district trustees visited the villages to familiarize themselves with the settings, no concerns were raised about their travel costs. By 1979, when the new Gitga'at school was officially completed, the principal, who was Ts'msyen and active in initiating the building of a new school, succeeding in getting some of the monthly district principals' meeting held in the village.

TS'MSYEN CURRICULUM AND SM'ALGYAX LANGUAGE

In March 1978, even before the official 1979 transfer of authority, school board minutes record a unanimous motion:

> That the district staff continue an immediate survey of the three villages, Port Simpson, Kitkatla and Hartley Bay, with a view to introducing or renewing native language programs in them in the fall of 1978-79 if the survey so indicates and that during the school year 1978-79 a similar survey be conducted in the Prince Rupert attendance area.[40]

Along with this hopeful statement, there are also entries labeling First Nations students as deficient and in need of special assessments for learning disabilities and reading readiness.

40 Just prior to and during the period 1972 to 1979 the only other references in the school board minutes to the Ts'msyen students were the need for additional teachers on a seasonal basis in Port Edward (on the outskirts of the city of Prince Rupert) to accommodate children whose families came to town to work in the Port Edward cannery. Visits of district specialists to village schools to do reading and learning disability assessments are also noted during this period.

The language in these official documents is consistent with Canada-wide discourses, which construct difference as needing remediation (Abele, Dittburner, & Graham, 2000).

NEW INSTITUTIONAL DEVELOPMENTS

Significant structural changes in provincial fiscal arrangements, representation in local decision making and in teacher education have supported Indigenous educational reform.

FISCAL ARRANGEMENTS

As in the past, fiscal arrangements between the Department of Indian Affairs and the B.C. Ministry of Education were managed under the Master Tuition Agreement, and required calculation of a per capita grant that DIA transfers to the ministry, and the ministry in turn transfers to the district. However, province-wide lobbying by First Nations groups, in particular the First Nations Education Council, successfully established a Partnership Agreement and a program of "targeted funding" that now more powerfully positions First Nations in the processes of distributing funds.

FIRST NATIONS REPRESENTATION IN DISTRICT DECISION MAKING

Since the early years of the transfer of authority from federal to provincial authorities, First Nations in the north coast have continued their advocacy. The First Nations Education Council, with representatives from the local First Nations communities and from the school district, is central to educational governance in the Prince Rupert district. This council initiated and supports all the programs and curricula inclusive of First Nations histories and cultures developed in the last fifteen years.[41] It also officially

---

41 The First Nations Education Council includes First Nations representatives from each of the three villages, and the city of Prince Rupert as well as the village principals, the Northcoast Tribal Council, the Ts'msyen Tribal Council, the Friendship House, the Board of School Trustees, the District Superintendent, the First Nations Education Consultant, the First Nations Provincial Secretariat, and an elementary and secondary school principal from the city of Prince Rupert.

represents the collective interests of First Nations students vis-à-vis the Ministry of Education. Through the Master Tuition Agreement, the Department of Indian Affairs contracts directly with the province of B.C. to fund education for First Nations students. This arrangement bypasses local First Nations representation. The First Nations Education Council, through a partnership agreement/accountability contract with the school district, powerfully inserts First Nations voices into the dialogues about educational needs and priorities.[42] (Details of the October 2001 partnership agreement with the Prince Rupert School District can be viewed at *www.sd52.bc.ca/fnes/council.html*. Retrieved September 18, 2007.)

In addition, arrangements for a variety of special programs regarding First Nations language and culture and students' needs are funded by targeted (rather than ongoing) funding grants from the B.C. Ministry of Education. These targeted funds, which are also from DIA, are subject to annual reviews where the district must report how the monies were used and, where relevant, impacts on students' accomplishments. In Prince Rupert, reports go directly to the ministry and to the First Nations Education Council.

Selected details of the programs successfully initiated with the support and involvement of the council are outlined in the introduction to Chapter 9, which focuses on educational innovations in Sm'algyax language and Ts'msyen culture. The First Nations Education Council is supported in its work by the Ts'msyen Tribal Council (formed in 1988). This regional political group, formed principally to prepare for treaty negotiations, also has responsibilities in health, housing, and economic development. In 1980, its precursor, the North Coast Tribal Council, approached Simon Fraser University teacher-educators to work collaboratively with them and the district to develop a teacher education program to prepare fully credentialed First Nations teachers.[43]

---

42 In the current fiscal arrangement between the Department of Indian Affairs and the B.C. Ministry of Education, the ministry calculates a per capita grant that DIA transfers to the ministry and the ministry in turn transfers to the district.

THE FIRST NATIONS COMMUNITY-BASED TEACHER EDUCATION PROGRAM

Consistent with the discourse of local control, the teacher education program jointly constructed by the North Coast Tribal Council, Simon Fraser University, School District #52, and Northwest Community College was situated in Prince Rupert, rather than on the distant university campus in the Vancouver suburb of Burnaby.[44] Like similar programs in other Canadian provinces, this program responded to the desire for local control, as well as government requirements for professional teacher certification. This location made it possible for many of the student teachers to live at home with their families during the five-year full-time program.[45] Others, who did relocate to the regional center, were still closer to their homes in coastal villages or in Haida Gwaii than they would have been if required to attend at the Burnaby campus.

Rather than requiring student teachers to cut ties with their communities, it was possible to create new spaces where teachers could creatively construct their identities in unique ways that drew upon their linguistic and cultural practices,

43 At this time the council was the Northcoast Tribal Council and also included representatives from Haida Gwaii (the Queen Charlotte Islands).

44 During the third cohort the province created the University of Northern British Columbia that had, from its inception, a program in First Nations Studies (including a mandate to provide academic course work in First Nations languages). This new university is located in Prince George and Prince Rupert is one of the regions that it serves. Through their auspices SFU students were able to participate in UNBC linguistics courses in Sm'algyax. The work of UNBC regional coordinator and anthropologist Margaret Seguin Anderson was pivotal in facilitating this connection.

45 Some of the students had already completed some university transfer work at Northwest Community College. The Department of Indian Affairs) allocates funds to individual bands for distribution to students wishing to enroll in post-secondary education. These tuition funds are not unlimited, and band education authorities are empowered to make selections among applicants, especially when funds allocated in a particular year are not sufficient to provide for all applicants. With continuous increases in the numbers of applicants for post-secondary education funding, bands must annually demonstrate to DIA their needs for increases in funding.

as well as practices of mainstream educators (Stairs,1993; Wyatt, 1978/79).[46] In a period of approximately fifteen years, three cohorts of approximately twelve students each met requirements for provincial teacher certification. They also completed an academic minor in linguistics, and all of these courses used Sm'algyax for illustrative material. Six months of classroom practice were completed in local schools. A graduate of the first cohort supervised the second and third cohorts.

This community-based teacher education program is rooted in the philosophy formally and explicitly articulated in the National Indian Brotherhood policy paper, Indian Control of Indian Education (1972). While the initial National Indian Brotherhood (NIB) vision of reconfigured education focused centrally on a metamorphosis in the experiences of new generations of First Nations children, it is apparent that the experiences of the First Nations teachers themselves speak of educational metamorphosis. National discourses of curriculum reform sustain affirm and support many First Nations educators in their creative work.

Proposed reforms have the potential to reposition teachers from the periphery of the mainstream educational community into more central positions as educational and social activists. In these more central positions, they can bring curriculum and programs to education that build on the multifaceted aspects of their identities. However, before they can do this activist work, they must secure employment. In their struggles and successes finding jobs, they are brought face to face with professional association/union discourses. These are chronicled in the vignettes in the next chapter.

---

46 In contemporary sociocultural theory, these spaces are identified as "third spaces" (Bhaba, 1996). Teachers can select from discourses of indigenous and mainstream cultures in constructing classroom experiences.

Chapter 6:
The World of Employment:
Finding a Job

They say they are supposed to hire First Nations teachers first, but I don't know. There are fifty-five qualified teachers on the substitute list. They are all looking for jobs in this city too. I'd be ticked off if I had been teaching for ten years, applied for a job, and they hired a first-year First Nations teacher instead. I'd like to get a job, but I don't want to push anyone out who has been there for ten years. That's why I'm looking at a second option: curriculum development. (Isabelle)

Teachers had a variety of experiences in their job searches. Immediately after graduating from the SFU teacher education program, Maureen got a job in the band-controlled school in her home community of Old Massett in Haida Gwaii, where she continues to work.[47] Bea, well established in Prince Rupert with her husband and children, could only find work in the village of Lax Łgu'alaams (Port Simpson), which employed approximately twelve teachers at the time.[48] She lived with her in-laws during the week when she was teaching, and flew home to Prince Rupert for the weekends. She did this for several years before taking a leave from teaching, and then securing a position

---

47 In Haida Gwaii, First Nations students may attend either band-controlled or public schools. Maureen immediately got a job teaching primary grades in the small band-controlled school in the village of Old Massett. She later assumed the position of head teacher in this three-teacher school. Students from Old Massett also attended the provincial school a few kilometers closer to the town of Massett.

48 In general, teachers have relatively less difficulty in securing positions in village schools. There tend to be proportionally more job openings in these schools than in the city schools. Newcomers to the profession commonly fill vacancies. Most often (and there are some notable exceptions), the novices stay in these positions only until they are successful in filling a vacancy in the city. As far back as 1907, the village of Hartley Bay had difficulty retaining teachers

in the city-based public school First Nations elementary program.[49] She now teaches elementary grades in a community school in Prince Rupert specially designated to provide a burgeoning number of services and programs linking school and families. Nadine, unable to find work at the six-teacher school in her home village of Hartley Bay, spent a period of time on the Prince Rupert teacher-on-call (TOC) list before securing a newly created position to teach Sm'algyax language in Prince Rupert secondary schools.[50]

The vignettes in this chapter, which focus on the period after teachers completed their certification, document situations when everything fell into place, as in Cam's immediate employment in his home village, as well as experiences where getting a job was a struggle (Isabelle and Pansy's vignettes). The struggles (Bakhtin, 1991) were with mainstream union discourses regarding seniority and the hiring practices which these set in motion. The vignettes also relate the teachers' creativity in dealing with the barriers to employment.

STRUGGLES IN EMPLOYMENT DISCOURSES

The ideology of local control of education, articulated in the National Indian Brotherhood's Indian Control of Indian Education policy paper, emphasized the importance of employing First Nations teachers. This idea is challenged by the authoritative policy discourses of unions that prevail in the world of public school employment.[51] The federal reform

49 This program, more fully described in Chapter 9, is for students in Grades 5 and 6. It emphasizes integration of a strong focus on Ts'msyen culture, with the provincial curriculum. The enrollment is kept low (between twelve and fifteen) in order to allow for more one-to-one student teacher interaction than is ordinarily possible.

50 Many beginning teachers – or teachers new to a district – commonly work as teachers-on-call (TOC), filling in for absent teachers before they secure full-time employment. Districts often use this practice as a way of getting to know applicants before they hire them for full-time positions.

51 Beynon's 1991 study of employment of First Nations teacher education graduates indicated that employment rates of First Nations teachers are higher for communities that have band-controlled schools.

initiative of employment equity (Abella, 1984; Government of Canada, 1986), gives priority to qualified applicants of Aboriginal and visible minority ancestries, as well as women and individuals with disabilities. While this policy is upheld in nationally administered and funded institutions, it is not part of either the local school district or the province-wide teachers' union employment policies.[52]

The world of public school employment is what Holland (1998) calls a cultural or "figured" world. Like other worlds, such as the village or the classroom, this figured world has its own authorized ways of speaking and acting with compelling implications for teachers' identities. It is mainly the provincial teachers' federation that dictates these authorized ways of speaking and acting. The official discourses – the rules and regulations of both provincial and local branches of the British Columbia Teachers' Federation – can block entry to the figured world of public school teaching. They interfere with possibilities for taking up hard-won teacher identities. These discourses establish the terms for appointments, job security, and lay-off, including "bumping" by more senior colleagues. The "last hired, first fired" job security rule is an example of a professional/ union authoritative discourse that undercuts First Nations teachers' chances for securing the positions they need in order to advocate for the people in their communities. Details of how these discourses play out in the Prince Rupert district are outlined in the next section.

---

52 Federal employment equity policies apply to federal employers and any agency or institution that receives more than $200 000 per year in government grants or contracts. Provincial school districts receive no federal funds for their regular programs. However, federal Department of Indian Affairs money goes to the provincial ministry of education to be spent on behalf of First Nations, i.e. the Master Tuition Agreement.

EMPLOYMENT DISCOURSES IN THE
PRINCE RUPERT SCHOOL DISTRICT

Policies regarding seniority govern many aspects of hiring. This official discourse comes into operation if district enrollments decline, or if class sizes are increased. In the Prince Rupert district, where the economy is resource-based on logging and fishing, cyclical economic fluctuations are quickly reflected in school enrollments as families (mostly non-Aboriginal) seeking or losing employment, move in and out of the region. Class size increases, contractually negotiated between the school district and the teachers' union, have resulted in a decrease in the overall number of employed teachers.[53]

While the elementary school enrollments of Aboriginal students in Prince Rupert have remained the same or increased, declining enrollments of non-Aboriginal students can lead to the layoff or underemployment of First Nations teachers who are the relative newcomers to the profession. Additionally, a more senior teacher returning from educational or maternity leave might take priority over a First Nations teacher with fewer years of district seniority.

Through continual participation in the discourse of seniority and its attendant notions of what is fair, the discourse became internally persuasive for Isabelle. Her comment at the beginning of this chapter illustrates her acceptance of seniority policies. However, as she describes in the vignette "They say they need more First Nations teachers" she creates ways to keep herself motivated and productive. In the vignette "At first I was excited . . . but now it looks grim." Pansy describes her discouragement and frustration at losing her position teaching First Nations studies in secondary school. Like Isabelle, she finds other educational work to help her maintain her identity as a teacher.

---

53 This negotiating strategy was widely used to offset increases in teachers' salaries. Higher salaries led to fewer teachers being employed and larger class sizes for those with jobs.

In addition to their individual efforts to build their teacher identities, the teachers are supported by the First Nations Education Council, which is chipping away at structural impediments to employment by creating opportunities for the First Nations educational discourses that these teachers can bring into the figured worlds of the schools. Working with district officials and curriculum specialists, the council has created employment opportunities for teachers who not only meet all provincial certification requirements, but also have additional qualifications related to their knowledge of Sm'algya̱x language and Ts'msyen culture and preparation to bring them into the curriculum.[54] The council is articulating a pathway between employment equity and Indian control discourses on the one hand, and mainstream policy discourses of district and teachers' federation on the other. In turn, their creativity clears a space for teachers to create new definitions of what it means to be a First Nations teacher in mainstream schools. The Role Model Program, curriculum development initiatives, the district-wide Sm'algya̱x language programs (each described more fully in Chapter 9) have all created new openings for First Nations teachers to bring their discourses and identities into the figured world of teaching.

Sometimes dispirited in their search for employment, teachers nevertheless responded to the obstacles that they encountered with energy and creativity. The frustrations they describe were transitory, as they (and their predecessors from earlier cohorts who serve in positions of leadership in the district) improvised new practices and programs to tackle long-standing obstacles to their participation. These programs are concrete evidence that development of a First Nations program infrastructure has worked effectively to provide employment opportunities. Thus the entire burden of change has not been left on the shoulders of individual teachers (McCarthy, 1990).

---

54 In some literature on employment of minority teachers in public districts' concerns are articulated about whether these teachers are becoming ghettoized if they are unable to easily secure non-specialist, i.e., regular enrolling classroom positions, or positions in classrooms with few minority students (Gordon, 2000; Osler, 1997).

In this chapter, the focus is on the world of employment. However, getting a job, as critical as it is in bringing about change, is simply the threshold to the figured worlds of village and classroom, each with its own discourses, practices, obstacles to and opportunities for the on-going development of teachers' professional identities. These will be considered in subsequent chapters.

They say they need more First Nations teachers - Isabelle

There are plans to incorporate First Nations language (Ts'msyen) curriculum next year (by September 1995) and that's what I want to work at, because that's what we've been doing already as we prepare our curriculum for the classroom. I'm on the school district First Nations Education Council, I'm involved in learning the language, and I like to write. In fact, my cousin – who is a good illustrator – worked with me, and we wrote a couple of books for our classes. We've all written books and been encouraged to get them published. I have lots of good ideas, things I've wanted to work on for a couple of years: language learning, working with elders. That's what I'd like to do if I don't get a full-time teaching job. (June 1994, immediately after completing the teacher education program.)

Six months later

I'm a teacher-on-call, and I'm on the First Nations role model program. I've had quite a lot of work: I got eight and a half days last month and two already so far this month, which is good. I'm mostly in the same school, where I feel really comfortable. I know it is probably better to say that you'll teach any grade in any school, but I told them I'm really familiar with Roosevelt and Seal Cove, and I've gotten lots of work there. Pansy has also been asking for me in her class as a member of the Role Model Program to teach Ts'msyen. She has the Futures, Kickstart, and Quest programs for the students that aren't in the school system. There is a wide range of them from fourteen to fifty, all wanting to get their Grade 12 diplomas. The experience is good. Every class you go into, you learn something.

I applied for a job at Roosevelt last week. I didn't get it because of lack of teaching experience. I needed to have more of a background in psychology, because there were students in the class with severe behavior problems. I've tried to get psychology courses twice, even by correspondence, but they've been full. They're hard to get into. It wasn't a job to get right into for a first-year teacher anyway.

Meanwhile, I'm doing a lot of things that I never got to do while I was taking the teacher education program. I'm playing women's soccer and basketball. I help at Roosevelt as a parent with after-school events. I'm on their advisory board and working committee, which is good. I help at their bingos and at Seal Cove's too. I help with the Kitkatla village dance group. We started in town here. When the kids from the village come here for school they miss the dancing from home, so I lined up a place for them, and we practice every Thursday. There are thirty kids who come out and have a good time every week. We've been invited to a dance for a youth gathering this week for their opening ceremonies.

I applied for another job as a Sm'algyax language curriculum developer. They wanted a fluent person and someone qualified to teach. I had to build my case, mentioning what I taught during my practicum and in the Role Model Program. I'm not fluent, but I'm functional in Sm'algyax. I explained all that, but it wasn't enough. They ended up hiring a non-native person who was qualified to develop curriculum but knew nothing about the language. I was willing to learn from working my way up, one grade at a time. However, I didn't get it. Then I applied for another job as a curriculum implementer at the resource centre. One of the qualifications that they asked for was experience conducting training for teachers in this district to offer the Ts'msyen language. I didn't get it because of lack of teaching experience. Once again, it went to a non-native; not even a local. I can't see how that person is going to in-service district teachers here on the Ts'msyen reading series. I was short-listed for a job at the Friendship Centre, but someone else got that one.

Internal listings are not really fair. This year they have the same two teachers they had last year for First Nations Studies 12 at the high schools. I know some people who are now qualified to teach secondary, and they don't really have a chance at these jobs because of internal listings. Pansy went in as a teacher-on-call to a couple of First Nations 12 classes and learned that those kids weren't happy with their teacher. I can't understand why they hire the same people when there are qualified First Nations people to teach now.

I would have gotten a job if I had been prepared to teach in the Kitkatla village school, but I didn't want to. I have cousins up in the Skeena River, and they said there were job openings there. They wanted my résumé. I just can't live in the village. I grew up in the city. I don't think I would move to get a job. My daughter is in her last year of elementary, and next year she'll be in high school and I just can't move her anywhere. She's at an age and grade where it would not be good to move her. As for me, I can't see myself living anywhere but here; especially not in the village. It is too small and too far away.

Right now I'm taking a writing correspondence course through a writing school in Ottawa. I just got a bursary, which should cover a computer, printer, discs, and paper. A second career choice! (December 1995)

A year and a half after completing teacher education

I expected to get a job right away, because they're always saying how badly they need First Nations teachers. There's such a high proportion of First Nations students here. I applied for a few jobs but I didn't get them because of lack of experience. I found out that you have to work with the union rules and be waiting on an internal list. I've already been on the teacher-on-call list for two years, and it's not getting any shorter. I've heard that there are thirty-five qualified teachers on it right now. The ones that make the sacrifice and go out of town like my cousin Bea can get a job and get some experience. Now she has a better chance than me of being hired in the city. I still don't think I can do that. It is really hard for me to move away and work in a village, because I have a daughter, thirteen, who will be in high school next year. At Grade 10, she would have to come back here anyway. (June 1996)

(The following year, Isabelle got a part-time position teaching in the Ts'msyen language program. This was later increased to four days a week.)

At first I was excited...but now it looks very grim - Pansy

At first, the prospect of being a teacher was really exciting, but now that I'm job seeking it looks very grim. I expected to be hired immediately, but unfortunately it doesn't happen that way. I did my practicum at the Grade 2/ 3 level, and I was expecting I would get a primary level teaching job. However, I'm also really interested in becoming more knowledgeable as a First Nations counselor or First Nations studies teacher for Grades 11 and 12. They don't have these positions in Masset or Haida Gwaii yet. If I could get into either one of those positions, I could start building the foundation to implement it into our own curriculum on the islands (Haida Gwaii). Since this one in Prince Rupert is still a pilot project, it is a good time to start working in the program. I have my adult instructor diploma, and I'm working on a major in First Nation Studies. I almost have my Post Baccalaureate Diploma. I have good qualifications to go into the high school and teach First Nations studies. However, it is highly unlikely that I will get that job.

There are fifty-five teachers right now on the teacher-on-call list. Even though I've sent in my résumé, there is only a very slim chance that I will be considered for these jobs this year, so I'll just continue to be a teacher-on-call at all grade levels. I'm anxious to work, I know I'm qualified, I'm excited, and at this stage I'm saying, "just give me a job." Right now the union has even capped the teacher-on-call list. There are too many on the list, and it's hard to even get called. From January to May I've had a maximum of three days per month.

Right now I'm taking three courses which will complete my Post Baccalaureate, and I'm also on the district Role Model Program. I've got a lot on my agenda. I want to do my master's degree, I want to write a book about my grandmother, I want to teach. I wish I had had this ambition ten or twelve years ago. (June 1995)

Six months after completing teacher education

I'm teaching First Nations studies full-time at the Friendship Centre for three different groups. It is a four-month contract, so I'll do the best I can for that time and then look for a regular teaching job. I teach the Futures students who are seventeen and under, and can't make it through the regular system; the Quest students who are over seventeen, and the Kickstart Program, which is all adults. I feel good about being able to teach them about what I know. I like being able to put my own curriculum together; there is often nothing available. I have to modify it to suit the needs of each of the three groups. The Kickstart Program is really good. All the students are adults; mature and pretty eager to learn, but with the Futures' kids it is hard to keep them focused and motivated. Some students didn't fit into the high school system . You have to be very energetic to keep them involved. The Quest students are mature also, and although you have to be patient, they're very good students. I teach First Nations studies to all three groups, and there are two other teachers who teach them math, science, socials, computers, and life skills. (December 1995)

Two years after completing teacher education:
Seniority overrules

My goal in life was to become an educator. I started off getting early childhood and business management certificates, which allowed me to teach pre-school and operate my own gift shop. However, I wanted to teach in the public school system, and after many years I accomplished my dream. In doing this, I became a role model for my own and many other First Nations children. It took six solid years to complete a degree in general studies, an adult instructor diploma, and finally a master's in curriculum and instruction, my ultimate goal. The only way to complete my master's was to move to the city, which my husband and I did. During that time, there were many stressful moments, deadlines to meet, assignments to be completed, and all-night study sessions. I was dedicated and determined. I worked hard, maintained a positive attitude, and with the support of my family, was able to complete this milestone in my life. I was excited about the new path that was opening; teaching children and adults was my long awaited dream.

I started teaching right away at the First Nations Education Center. I taught First Nations studies to college students and alternate classes. It was exciting to teach adults, because they returned to school by choice and were eager and willing to learn. After my contract there was over, I moved into the public system working as a teacher-on-call and as a program implementer for First Nations Education Services. It was an exciting and challenging position. I was familiar with the process, so I could do without daily supervision or instructions.

Next came the highlight of my teaching career. I was hired as First Nations counselor and teacher of First Nations studies at the local secondary school. I held this position for two consecutive years. I felt that I had strengths and assets I could bring to the job: my knowledge of northwest coast First Nations peoples and my personal and professional background. Having been a band council member for twelve years, I was well prepared to teach such topics as the Indian Act, band council systems, treaty process, and how to analyze, critique, and defend complex issues such as self-government and land claims. I had grown up in the oral tradition with songs and dances, and this was a powerful asset combined with my educational training. I carve out of argillite and wood, and teach the art of button blankets, drum making, and dance regalia. I have a strong passion for storytelling, and use this art as a pedagogical bridge to teach students their history, identity, and traditions. Working from the oral tradition in my teaching gave students confidence and self-esteem. They became more appreciative of their heritage and developed a greater understanding of their history. It was exciting to witness their growth as they became increasingly confident in their abilities to learn their culture and history.

In the two years I was there, I captured the students' and teachers' admiration. They respected my professional abilities, I felt welcome in the school, and I thrived teaching at that level. I was offered and accepted a position to teach First Nations art 9/10, and eagerly added this to my position teaching First Nations studies 12. However, my teaching career was soon shattered by a district process of "bumping", which I had not been prepared for personally or professionally.

Bumping is part of the collective agreement that allows seniority to overrule everything else. It occurs when student enrollment declines and staffing reductions are deemed to be necessary to meet the district budget commitments. Notices are sent out to schools, a surplus declaration is issued, and the teachers with the least seniority are declared surplus. The surplus declarations had been issued across the district in accordance with the teachers' union and Board, and that a teacher with greater seniority could take my position. I had been aware that this could happen, but had felt confident that I would keep my position. However, the next day the principal and a union representative called me into the office to inform me that I was bumped.

When I received the news I was devastated. Naturally, I questioned my own abilities. It seemed so degrading and humiliating to have gone to school for so many years to become a professional teacher and then to get bumped by another First Nations teacher. I feel this whole process is unfair for any new teacher, and unfortunately they have to go through it until they gain enough seniority to hold a permanent position. I strongly believe that if the hiring decision had been left up to the principal and a subcommittee from the First Nations Education Council, I would still have my teaching position.

Many teachers were sympathetic and empathized with my situation. Many students were angry, sad, and heartbroken.

Some parents told me that they finally had a teacher they could trust and work with, and now they would have to start all over again. It is the First Nations students who ultimately suffer from this process, because of lack of continuity.

I wrote a letter requesting another evaluation of my qualifications, because these are supposed to be taken into account along with seniority in the bumping process. Also, as a member of the First Nations Education Council, I am aware that its goals are to maintain continuity in First Nations education positions, and to hire teachers who have considerable knowledge in local content. I strongly believe that I was more qualified for this position, and in my letter, I outlined why I thought I was a stronger candidate. I gave the following reasons:

I am committed to remain in this position and provide continuity for the next eight years. I have dedicated my time and energy to developing a book for First Nations studies 12 focusing on northwest coast First Nations people and recognizing the cultural protocol of the Ts'msyen people. I have taken the initiative to learn the basics of the Sm'algyax language and have incorporated it into the First Nations 12 course. I am a functional Haida speaker, which allows me to compare and contrast First Nations peoples' unique languages. This is valuable for the language component of the course.

I am trusted, and have built strong rapport with many students, teachers, and parents. They see me as a professional who provides support and advice, and as someone they can talk to about confidential issues. To them, I am a role model and an educational advocate who encourages their students to stay in school. I have established a strong, positive working relationship with the other two counselors, and we work closely together. I am a team player and work well with other teachers and staff members.

I have taken over forty hours of the new computer training in preparation for the change over next year. I have attended and continue to attend many workshops and conferences to increase my personal and professional knowledge. I have developed the First Nations 12 curriculum and been in the position for two years. A number of students have only taken part of it, planning to do the rest next year. My leaving will break the continuity and the students will be unable to take all of the required core units for First Nations studies 12. First Nations students have been suffering from this lack of continuity for years; there have been six different teachers in the position since its inception. I am highly qualified to teach First Nations art 9/10. My background knowledge and skills include making button blankets, drums, dream catchers, carving, painting plaques and paddles, basket weaving, and beadwork. I have a master's degree in curriculum and instruction. I have taken students on a number of field trips, and begun several projects which will be lost if I am bumped. The notice I received said:

> Please remember that teachers have to bump into positions if they are to have a job in the fall. Support your colleagues by welcoming teachers who have been forced to change schools and bump into a position. It will be equally important to support the teachers who are bumped, and as a consequence declared surplus. This support can help make a negative, stressful experience more bearable.

I had two days to make a decision as to whether I should use my seniority and bump another teacher. There were nineteen positions that I was eligible for, eleven located in three outlying villages. My immediate response was that I could not relocate to a village, and the other positions were for French or Sm'algyax language. I decided I did not want to exercise my seniority to bump another teacher, so I chose to be on the recall list.

I was ironically caught up in this system where seniority dominates, and I don't believe my qualifications were taken into serious consideration. This whole stressful process has prompted many questions. Why did I go through all this education only to be bumped out of my teaching and counseling position? Was it worth it? Would it have hurt less if a non-native teacher had bumped me? Is it fair that the teacher who bumped me didn't consider my feelings and aspirations? After going through a roller coaster of emotions, I have come to the conclusion that the prospect of becoming a professional teacher is grim and discouraging when faced with the bumping process. However, on a positive note, some of my teacher friends and colleagues did not have to go through this heartbreaking process, because they chose to teach in villages that were their home communities. A couple of teachers have allies and family who gave them support in securing a teaching position in their home ocmmunity.

Meanwhile, my life must go on. I have to keep an open mind and a happy spirit. I must continue to hope that I will get another teaching position I enjoy, or return to the one I just left. One teacher said, "One door closes and another one opens." My friend and fellow counselor said, "This is the beginning of an even better avenue." I know my friends are consoling me, but I have trained all my life in the traditions of our people, and I have spent so many years at university to now have my teaching position destroyed. In my opinion, this process of placing seniority above qualifications is grossly unfair. This is my first experiene in the bumping process. I empathize with other teachers who have to go through this process. (June 1997)

Going home is bliss - Cam

The community that I am teaching in is home to me, and working and living here is a dream come true. I was born and raised here, and I just came right back in. It was almost like one of those sets of Lego: it just fit together and was perfect. It is what I always wanted to do. I always wanted to make a living here. To be completely honest, teaching wasn't my first choice, but it worked out perfectly and I am enjoying it. I know everybody here; I'm practically related to half of the village either through blood or marriage, and I fit right in. These are the people I want to be with, and I feel that I'm actually getting something across to the kids. I went to school with their parents, and it is amazing to me how I can see the relationships, understand the thinking. The whole experience is just so personal for me and I'm almost in ecstasy. When I finish work at the school I walk out the door and I am in the village: where I want to be. I've got a steady income, and I'm still not used to the fact of getting paid for this. My lunch is ready when I come home. I'm comfortable, and happy and I've got my little girl now. It is just so beautiful and it is exactly what I wanted it to be.

I graduated in 1986 from secondary school in Prince Rupert and I've gone back to Hartley Bay every chance I've had. I don't feel right anywhere else. I've only been out three times this whole year. My little girl is the same way. These last couple of days we've been in Rupert, and she just hasn't been herself. She is in an environment that is not hers, and that is how I felt the whole of those ten years I was away. I kept in contact with my mom and dad, who always taught at the school. I always knew what was going on, and I always wanted to go back.

Another big plus for me was that my wife and I went through our education together. Before we took the teacher education program, I already had two years of university. I didn't really know what I wanted to do at that point, but I always had in mind that I wanted to get home. I'm really close to my mom and dad and my grandparents, and I didn't want to be away from them. I had good grades and I was getting funded, and I thought if I kept going, things would hopefully fall into place. At first I took an aquaculture course when the industry was booming, because I figured I could get a job afterwards, but it didn't pan out. Then I got my welding ticket, because I thought it would help me out when I'm fishing. In fact, I still plan on fishing in the summertime on our boat. Then this teacher education course came along, and it just put everything into perspective. My wife and I both got in and took off from there. Those years I was in the program I just kept waiting for something bad to happen, because I am that sort of person. I think that if everything is going well, you have to keep an eye over your shoulder because something is bound to hit you, and it hurts the worst when everything is going well. Even during the practicum, I kept waiting for the ceiling to fall in, but it never did. It was perfect. I had two of the best school associates you could ever ask for, and a good school.

It's June now, and I've got four weeks of teaching left in this school year. My relationships with staff and family are all becoming more solid, because everybody knows me and I know them. These kids are being taught by someone they know will always be in Hartley Bay, and that's a vital change from having teachers who spend two years in the village and then move on. You have to just keep on going and watch the little successes mount up and ultimately make a big hill. (June 1996)

SUGGESTED DISCUSSION QUESTIONS

1. What strategies and discourses did the individuals in these vignettes use to deal with the obstacles to employment that they encountered? What other positions did they occupy that they used to build their skills and educational perspectives? How did the strategies they employed both reflect and develop their identities as teachers of First Nations ancestry?

2. What structural changes in hiring policies or in school programs would facilitate employment of First Nations teachers? How can new hiring or curriculum policies open up more positions for First Nations teachers? Might these have any negative consequences?

3. Recall a situation when you feel that you have been treated unjustly. Describe the situation; write about what helped you in dealing with this situation. What was helpful immediately? What was helpful as time passed? If, as Hall says, "identities are always in process," what implications did this experience have for your identity as a participant in a cultural community and as a teacher?

4. What are the challenges when everything just "clicks"? How does it affect your outlook on people who are having difficulties?

CHAPTER 7:
COMMUNITIES AND PARENTS

When I first moved back [to the village] some people were uncomfortable with me around. One night, I went to a function and some guy sitting at a table we joined said, "Oh there's a teacher here. I am not going to stay." Then he actually got up and left. Shortly after that, we went to another outing and he was there and I just told him: "You know, I am not different because I am a teacher. I eat, drink, and sleep just like everybody else. I just have a different job than you. I am not better than you, and you are not better than me. I am just a person here with a job, and my job happens to be teaching. Anyone who has children is a teacher. If you have kids, you are automatically put in the teaching position; you have to teach this child everything from birth to when they are adults, and then you still continue to teach them."

(Marilyn, October 1996)

THE DIVIDE BETWEEN THE SCHOOL AND THE COMMUNITY

Similar to Marilyn's experience, many of the vignettes in this chapter relate how First Nations community members can position First Nations teachers as allies of the school and alien to their communities. In "School is an easy target," Eva-Ann points out how community members in her village see the community and the school as two different worlds, like the "figured worlds" that Holland and colleagues (1998) describe. In part, this distancing is the legacy of the mission and residential school period, as well as the period of so-called integration into public schools. During these times, the practices of the school were imposed with the objective of eliminating the practices of the community. Some parents perceive a First Nations teacher who has succeeded in the world of schooling as a spokesperson for authoritative discourses of the residential, federal day school, or provincial public schools. They expect that this teacher will judge and blame them for their failures in school, learning difficulties their children may have, and for the other difficulties in their lives. They may also have hard feelings, because as Marilyn points out in the vignette "Working and living in your community," teachers are well-paid in communities where unemployment is high.

The variety of ways in which teachers respond to these negative perceptions illustrates that they understand how oppressive school experiences affect their communities. Knowing that they are perceived and positioned by many of their fellow community members as alien, they see that the initiative to build dialogue frequently rests with them. Marilyn, in the excerpt above, illustrates how she turned a negative encounter into an opportunity to reposition herself and insert the notions of equity and respect, rooted in Ts'msyen and Haida pedagogies, into her dialogues with parents. In this way, she opened the door to enlisting parents' support and making them collaborators in the project of redefining schooling.

BUILDING BRIDGES BETWEEN
THE WORLDS OF SCHOOL AND COMMUNITY

Teachers occupy positions both in the cultural worlds of their communities and their schools. Within the figured world of their community, teachers participate in a wide range of activities, including formal and informal clan, family, and village ceremonial gatherings (e.g., name-giving ceremonies); seasonal activities (e.g., fishing, hunting, and food preserving); public dance and drumming performances; and sports events at home or in other First Nations communities. Within the figured world of school and classroom, they participate in language programs, school-wide assemblies, district and province-wide curriculum initiatives, and conferences, as well as the daily implementation of provincial curriculum in language arts, math, and other curriculum areas.

Vignettes in this chapter illustrate teachers' dilemmas and delights in the noisy and messy process of constructing positive relations between these two figured worlds. They construct these relations by retaining connections to their diverse positions (as teacher, parent, clan member, and community member), rather than choosing between them. The multifaceted quality of their identities – connected to their multiple memberships – is a resource rather than contradiction. This is illustrated in the vignette "Teaching where you grew up," where Cam considers how important it is to him to coordinate his positions as a teacher and a member of local band government.

RESPECT IS THE FOUNDATION

As the teachers take the initiative to engage in conversations with parents and other community members, they can draw on ways of communicating that are well rooted in community traditions of learning. Respect is a central tenet in Indigenous pedagogies. Maureen, who returned as head teacher to the band-controlled school in Haida Gwaii, speaks in the vignette "Transforming attitudes" about the importance of maintaining respectful interactions with a coworker. She consistently did so even, when she felt her colleague was intent on disrupting her efforts to communicate openly with parents. In "You're treated right: it comes through the school," Cam reflects that his father, also a teacher, emphasized Ts'msyen values of respect in bringing the school and community closer together.

CHOOSING ADVOCACY AND DIALOGUE

In the following vignettes, teachers note how easily they could feel defeated by the range of community concerns that are the legacies of colonialism, such as substance abuse and child abuse. Nevertheless, they tenaciously continue their advocacy, and refuse to withdraw from the debates they encounter. Through their ongoing personal presence in the community, they create the links that draw parents into the world of the school.

Through dialogue, teachers begin to chip away at the old authoritative discourses of church and mainstream schools that devalued Indigenous ways of knowing and learning, and create "ever newer ways" to engage learners and their parents (Bakhtin, 1981, p. 346). Possibilities for initiating change rest in part with teachers' abilities to initiate new dialogues between participants in the figured worlds of school and community. In many of the vignettes, the dialogue is with the First Nations community. However, in the vignette "My position in the community," Marilyn succinctly points out how important it is for her to explain cultural practices to some of her non-First Nations colleagues.

The vignettes in this chapter articulate teachers' perspectives on the complexities and joys of creating the conversations that could help to knit together the disparate figured worlds of which they are members. In "Teaching in the village versus teaching in town," Bea relates the delights, in the village context, of easily bringing the two worlds of school and community together.

Building on and supporting the personal efforts of the teachers are substantial projects at an institutional level. These were initiated by the First Nations Education Council to draw parents into productive conversations regarding their children's education. These projects are documented in Chapter 9.

THE DIVIDE BETWEEN THE SCHOOL AND THE COMMUNITY

School is an easy target - Eva-Ann

In going back to my community, I think I knew how things would go. I think my expectations were pretty well right on. I get along well with a lot of the parents, and I was a little nervous about how some of them would feel towards me, because I thought they might look at me differently because of my teaching degree. I didn't know if they would think I was totally different because of that, that they wouldn't be able to get along with me because I was now affiliated with the school.

Some people bunch everything together with the school, and see the school and the community as two separate worlds. They don't try to join the two together. There have been a lot of bad feelings, and they like to blame the school for a lot of things [that are happening in the community].

I think it's just an easy target for most people to say, "This is what should be done there, and not at home." In fact, it should be done at home as well. Where there are issues with families and the school, the kids certainly know how to work the two, so they sort of clash. They know they can go home and tell their parents that something happened, when in fact it didn't happen that way. They know that their family will then go into the school and cause trouble. However, once they come up to the school and start talking with the teacher or the principal, everything starts to sort itself out. It's easy to say what we feel or what we think because we grew up with most of these parents, so that they know what we were like before we became teachers. Both my husband and I get along quite well with the community, and we are definitely part of the school, so we can work together between the two. (June 1996)

It's too hard - Nadine

Where I come from everyone is related; there's just so much family. You cross one child, and the whole family is down on you. It's too hard. It has happened to me before, and I just couldn't handle it. I kept teaching, but it was hard to see, hard to remain friends with the people in the community, because you hear everything they say about you. For me, it was just very discouraging. Village life is just so isolating. You can't get out when you want to. You can't just get away from everything, because you always know you have to go back.

If you go away it's a struggle to make the transition to being away, because you're used to having your family all around you. I've had my sisters come to town to stay with me for two weeks, and after two days they want to go home again. You just kind of get used to the boredom and the gossip, and you can't get away because you've been doing it for so long.

I know a lot of people who have come into town for counseling, and they've learned what it is they have to do to stop all that's happening in the village, but they just can't do it. They get caught right back up in it as soon as they go home. When I go to the village for a weekend, my head is spinning after three days; just listening to all that's been happening and knowing that it is all going to happen again, because nothing is being done about it. I am somewhat intimidating to them, because I was able to get out of that life. I'm not saying I'm better than anyone back there, but I know that I can now back away from the gossip. I can back away from everything now. I know how to do that. However, because I'm not teaching at home, everyone is my friend! They're all coming to talk to me, even though they know I've gone to school for those four years. It's weird, because one of my fellow teachers has gone through the same training as me, and yet they treat him like he thinks he is better than them because he is teaching there. They see him as someone who is in control of their children, and so they talk about him behind his back; they say everything to try and bring him down. Prince Rupert is a lot bigger. I prefer to teach in Rupert. You don't have to hear what everyone is saying about you: their sly remarks. You can go on living. You have so many friends to support you. I think it's sad that most of the kids don't know where they came from and what clan they're from, or where they belong. That makes me want to teach them. These kids need a lot more First Nations teachings than my people had; than the kids in the villages do. So that's my goal. (June 1996)

Working and living in your community - Marilyn

Working and living in the community is a lot different than I thought. I've actually had a really easy time of it. I've often noticed with First Nations people that when someone who hasn't had one for quite a while gets a job, the community doesn't support them. It's as if they would rather have them not working. If you're working, people say that you think you are better than everyone else. I saw that happen to a couple of First Nations teachers here who went through a really bad hassle.

In fact, one of them finally had to take some time off. However, it hasn't happened to me. I have very supportive parents in my class, and in the school for that matter. I think that the fact of my being First Nations has made them more comfortable talking to me than they would be to a non-First Nations teacher. It is partly because they have known me for years as a community member. They've known me as president of the parent advisory committee, and a lot of them came to talk to me about things that were going on with their children in the school. I think I've made a small dent as far as people coming to the school and feeling more comfortable there.

I still go out and continue to take part in all the community events: people see me. A couple of months ago, my husband and I went to a community dance where they were serving liquor. Everyone was really surprised that I was there, because teachers usually choose not to go when there is liquor involved. They were all saying, "What are you doing here?" My husband is a big part of the community, and it felt all right to me to go. I want to enjoy myself and see everybody. I wasn't drinking, but I wanted to visit with everyone. (June 1996)

BUILDING BRIDGES

Teaching where you grew up:
Serving your community through education - Cam

The parents grew up with me, and I think they are able to relate to what I am saying. They may not agree with it, they may argue with it, but at least they are willing to listen to me. Who knows, but maybe in a year from now when I talk to them, they will agree. I am not saying that I am right. I want to hear a lot more from them too. Hopefully together we can work closely to ensure that the kids make it through these grades, and are equipped with the tools necessary to carry out their schooling, get a job and to say "no" to those things which will hurt them. Hopefully we can work together to support kids in knowing what will help them through it all to be successful and to be proud of who they are. I can imagine what my teachers went through, because kids are always changing their minds about everything. What is important is to let them know that anything is possible. It's really tough that a lot of them have to see such bad things, but they need to know they can do whatever they want.

One thing I can't get used to is listening to a Grade 5 student say that she is going to leave the village for the weekend. When I ask, "Oh, are you going to go to Rupert?" She says: "Yeah, I have to go to counseling . . . " I wish I didn't know any Grade 5 that had to go to counseling, whether it be for sexual or physical abuse or whatever has happened to them. I know it has something to do with being brought up in the village, and it's too bad they have to go through it. I was more or less sheltered. My dad knew who to leave me with and my mom knew too, even though she was new to the community. I can't even fathom what those kids have had to deal with. That little girl who told me she had to go to counseling: it still rings in my head. These kids shouldn't even know what counseling is. They should just be worried about going swimming in June; having fun, not having to go and let someone listen to who has done what to them and relive the whole experience. It's just ugly.

I don't know what it all stems from. People were abused in residential schools, and then it carries on for generations. It just keeps going. It snowballs, and that's a tough one to deal with. We've had these social workers come into Hartley Bay with the idea of "changing all the savages" and showing us what is "right." They thought they could help by finding out who started it, who's been carrying on, who has hurt who. They thought they could bring it all out and change everybody in a summer. I've seen that happen twice in my life. But their approach was all wrong: they were going about it in all the wrong ways. They were just pouring salt on wounds that may be healing. It started to get really ugly. My dad was able to intervene, and talk to people, offer suggestions and sort of calm it down. He wasn't imposing his view, but he had seen the school turned upside down with this sort of thing before, and so he wanted to get er Seven 105

everything calmed down so that he could get on with the task at hand, while at the same time offering help to the people who wanted it. You can't help anybody who doesn't want it.

I am here for the same reason my dad was. I want to help. I am not trying to be an almighty power. I am not perfect. I just want to help. I went out and got educated. I know how to help. Don't run me into the ground for that. The people have elected me as Deputy Chief, but it's not power they've given me. The people are power. They put me where I am. I've got to serve them, and what better position could I be in to give help! In two years they can kick me out if they want: that's how long the term of office is. Even more, as far education goes, I know what needs to be done. I think I am being fair, and it is definitely a year of firsts for me. (June 1996)

RESPECT IS THE FOUNDATION

Transforming attitudes - Maureen

When I went back, I had a person assisting me who played a lot of mind games. It was very difficult, especially for my first year. There were a lot of things happening in the school and arrangements for various activities, and she was in the office to pick up the phone. She would get the messages, but she never relayed them to me. I was responsible for these kids. A lot happened that I needed to know about what they were supposed to be doing, but nothing was passed on. I bit my tongue and held on, and tried to show her a different way. I wanted to let her know that we could solve it in another way than hers, not by getting mad. I wanted to show her respect, and have her show me respect back. It took a while, and it took a lot of work, but it has sure helped this year. She is watching, and she wants to go into teaching now too. She wants to go in for a program where she will get her teaching degree. It was really hard, and I tried not to let it affect what was happening, for me and for the students. (October 1996)

You're treated right . . . it's come through the school - Cam

I've got so much respect for my mom and dad for what they've done. It's pretty close to thirty years since they came here with DIA, and they were the only teachers. Dad was born and raised here, and he could have done anything else, but he came back to Hartley Bay for the sole reason of making things better, or at least trying to. He's never given up on that. If my dad didn't still think he could make a difference, he wouldn't be here. They took so much bashing; especially my mom, because she's an outsider. She more than fits in there now, and everyone respects her. She sat on council for a good ten years, and has done a lot of work for the community. The people know that. I don't know if I would have been able to do what my dad did. I don't think I can measure up to what he has done, or is still doing as an educator, a principal, and as a community member. He is a truly unique man. I still don't know what drove him. He took so much abuse from his own people, calling him an "apple Indian": red on the outside, White inside. I don't know anybody who has a bigger heart for the people of Hartley Bay. He's done so much, and I think the school has played a very big part in the whole of village dynamics. When you walk into the Hartley Bay School, it's the same as when you walk off the plane. You're treated right. I've been around to a lot of villages, and there's not a more friendly place than here. I think a lot of it has come through the school. Not everybody is going to be a scholar that comes out of Hartley Bay School, but they are good people and they try. I can't ever imagine measuring up to what my father has done. He's brought such an important aspect of First Nations to teaching and being respectful to everyone. You can see it.

In everything he does and says, he has the kids from a First Nations community front and foremost. He manages to balance this with who he is as an administrator and educator in order to help the kids really appreciate the value of education, and yet never forget who they are and where they are from. I listen to friends in other villages who are afraid to go out after eight at night, and it makes me feel so good that Hartley Bay isn't like that. There may be people who disagree with me, but I think its like it is because of who has been in charge of the school. It's had a big impact on the kids I've grown up with. (June 1996)

CHOOSING ADVOCACY AND DIALOGUE

My position in the community - Marilyn

As a teacher in the community, I know I have some expectations of myself: of who I am to be. I don't go out partying because I know everyone is watching. I have to be an example of what not to do, because there's so much alcohol and abuse. I have to try to be positive. One of the things I can do is to help the other [non-first Nations] teachers to understand what is going on in the community. Just recently, there was a man in the community who passed away and it took the kids at least a week to recover from that. It was an extended family with a lot of family members, and so it affected not only all the kids, but their friends too. Being a role model also means learning to speak up. You need to have a voice. Action is where it's at. (2005)

Teaching in a village versus teaching in town - Bea

I really like the kids a lot. They're very affectionate and so easy to get along with. I find that different than in Rupert, in a way. Although the kids there were affectionate too, there seems to be more of a connection when you're in the village. In Rupert, always have to be prepared to explain to the parents what your concern is and what you are pleased about. In the village I feel a lot more accepted, and the children love studying about First Nations content with a First Nations teacher.

We are planning this big feast for a girl at the end of June, and we're all racing around doing projects for the feast. In fact, right now my class is making a miniature village to demonstrate how it looked historically. The feast is actually a celebration of our traditional technology. We're putting rocks on the seashore where people made their canoes. Gradually, the kids are learning that fire heated rocks were used in the process of canoe construction.[55]

In my opinion, in Prince Rupert, First Nations studies seem to happen mainly when there is a special event like the All Native Basketball Tournament. In the village, it is easier to get involved and include it on an ongoing basis. There's more access. You can just walk down to the beach. It's a natural thing to do. (June 1996)

---

55 Once the wood had been hollowed out with adzes, the canoe was filled with water and hot rocks. The steam that was created allowed the workers to widen the sides.

SUGGESTED DISCUSSION QUESTIONS

1. Have you ever been in a situation in which you felt you were mistrusted because of the position you occupied, rather than because of your words or your actions?

2. In your experience in First Nations communities, how do people develop respect for one another? What are the implications of kinship group membership and relationships? Does age play a part?

3. If education is central to the health of First Nations communities, why do First Nations teachers sometimes find that they are not respected by First Nations parents?

4. It is very common (both outside of and inside First Nations communities) for discourses of blame to develop. Teachers blame parents and parents blame teachers and the school for problems that arise. What historical factors contribute to this discourse? What are the limitations of approaching problems in this way?

5. What steps can be taken by First Nations teachers to effectively communicate and collaborate with parents? What kind of support might other groups in the community be able to contribute to building collaborative relations with parents?

6. What discourses can you draw upon to reposition yourself when you are not comfortable with how others have positioned you?

7. Individuals' discourses change in dialogue with others. How are teachers of First Nations ancestries uniquely positioned to initiate these dialogues? What kinds of dialogues can they initiate with parents? What kinds of discourses can they initiate with other teachers?

CHAPTER 8:
SCHOOLS AND CLASSROOMS,
COLLEAGUES AND KIDS

As a First Nations teacher, I was always anxious about being confronted by non-native parents wanting to know why we were involving First Nations content as teachers. No one ever did, but it was just a feeling. I didn't want to be explaining myself. (Bea)

When First Nations teachers reenter the world of schools – first as student teachers, and then as certified teachers – they are often in the minority, and "guests" in the space occupied by mainstream professionals. They know they are being measured and evaluated in relation to a cultural world and society that has historically devalued their languages and knowledge. Initially, they are disadvantageously positioned in the world of the school to initiate and sustain the conversations that could help to change these negative practices and perceptions. Nevertheless rests with them to take this initiative.

Not only do teachers need to advocate for themselves with their colleagues and administrators, advocacy is also an important part of the work they do for students and their parents. Sometimes the advocacy simultaneously addresses the need for teachers and students to work together to construct identities they all value. Advocacy is especially challenging when it calls laws into question (e.g., child protection laws) and Ministry of Education procedures for student assessment, which teachers perceive to undercut students' possibilities for constructing identities they value.

Finally, teachers need to advocate for their own children, and this presents dilemmas relating to the norms and authoritative discourses of professionalism articulated by the teachers' federation. Taking the initiative to move beyond advocacy and into dialogue is emotionally and intellectually demanding, especially when taken on in addition to the daily work of classroom teaching.

COLLEAGUES

When First Nations teachers take strong exception to daily, taken-for-granted practices in the schools, it rests with them to convey to their non-First Nations administrators and teaching colleagues why they feel so strongly. As illustrated in the vignette "Explaining it to colleagues: Giving voice to the echoes of the past," it falls to the First Nations teacher to paint a picture of the historical world of the residential school or the church-run day school. They need to explain how the legacy of this world continues to negatively affect parents and children.

Similarly, "Talking to learn" illustrates how Marilyn, positioned by her principal as a novice teacher, struggles to reposition herself in order to create safe spaces for her students. She asserts her authority about what teaching strategies are best for her students. Importantly, she found an oral approach, so central in Indigenous pedagogies, most effective. In "Healing the community" Deborah challenges the principal for avoiding issues of students' emotional well-being. In concurrence with Indigenous traditions, she knows that emotional security is key in creating an environment that nurtures learning.

WHAT IS BEST FOR THE KIDS?

In building relationships of trust with students, teachers may come into conflict both with the discourses of professional ethics and legal considerations. Official policies of attendance and evaluation and school rules about inappropriate behavior, suspensions, and expulsions can contribute to tensions in teachers' relationships with students and parents. As the teachers navigate these authoritative discourses in order to establish their positions and identities as professionals, they must also answer these discourses in ways that will support students in constructing their own identities.

PROFESSIONAL ETHICS / LEGAL CONSIDERATIONS / SCHOOL CODES OF CONDUCT

Teachers must decide how varied authoritative discourses – such as the professional code of ethics of the teachers' federation, legal protocols from the Ministry of Children and Families regarding child protection, school rules and regulations in codes of conduct – are implicated in their practices. In the vignette: "Joe's humiliating experience," advocating for the child and his parents involved providing them important insider information from the teachers' code of ethics. In the vignette "Sam's Story," the narrator implicitly discerns that formal legal discourses don't appear to serve the best interests of the children. Teachers find themselves needing to make discretionary judgments about discourses that authorize government or school authorities to protect and act for "their (First Nations') own good" and decide when these facilitate students' well being and when they obstruct it. If it is school rules that seem obstructive, it is also necessary to decide the best course of action, as in "Monica's Story." Determining how best to intervene with respect and care in cases where First Nations students are physically aggressive is also important (see "Julien's story") especially when school authorities caution otherwise (see"Judy and Tom's Story)."

STUDENT IDENTITIES

A key part of effective teaching lies in teachers' efforts to assist students, respectively, in constructing their identities. The teachers' identities and voices "half theirs and half someone else's" (Bakhtin, 1981, p. 345) – in this case, their students – can be mutually supportive, but it is often a considerable struggle to work out this kind of relationship (see "Freddy talks too much").

The systems of testing and evaluation teachers are obliged to administer often undercut their opportunities for establishing supportive relationships with students. Evaluation regimens and norms of school attendance are repeatedly documented as prominent tools in assigning marginal and devalued identities to these students (Varenne & McDermott, 1999).

Overall participation and completion rates for First Nations students in this district, as in other districts in the province and country where First Nations students are enrolled, are well below norms for the school population in general (First Nations Education Council & School District 52, 2005). How can teachers take up identities as effective educators who provide supportive learning environments with relevant teaching materials when students are so disaffected with the system that they have no desire to be in school? And yet First Nations teachers who work in this system can feel that their credibility will be undermined if they do not apply institutional norms regarding attendance and assessment equally to all students (see "Teddy's Final Year").

Finally, First Nations educators recognize that the normative discourses of "special needs": LD (learning disabled), ADD (attention deficit disorder), FAS (fetal alcohol syndrome), ESD (English second dialect) – as well as the specialist teacher designations associated with the labeling systems – all marginalize not only the labeled students, but also the teachers who work with them. Wherever the above named "special" or "alternate" programs exist, First Nations children comprise a disproportionate number of the students enrolled. (See vignette "Eddie's struggles"). The fact that these labels qualify the district for additional government funds makes it particularly difficult to challenge these programs. It is frustrating for teachers who see that government money would be better spent for programs that validate rather than stigmatize student and teacher identities.

TEACHER AS PARENT

Negotiating the official discourses of deficiency that construct First Nations students as "less than" in order to support them in constructing their identities is difficult work. What added complexities are there when teachers see their own children being treated unfairly? How can they voice their concerns as parents when their professional positions prohibit them from criticizing colleagues? (See the vignettes "That TOC" and "Clayton").

The contradictions and challenges posed to First Nations teachers in mainstream institutions and the ways that they negotiate these are vividly illustrated in the vignettes in this chapter. The vignettes also make it abundantly clear that these teachers are committed to their students' emotional, social, and intellectual well-being, and that this well-being is, above all else, their reason for teaching and working in their communities.

Chapter 9 documents programming that valorizes rather than stigmatizes First Nations cultural, community, and human resources. This kind of programming engages students so that school becomes lively and enjoyable, rather than a test of endurance.

PROFESSIONAL RELATIONSHIPS WITH COLLEAGUES

Talking to learn - Marilyn

When the principal was discussing his observations of my teaching with me, he said that my journal time was "too loose"; that there was too much talking. He said journal time was a personal sort of time. I replied that that might be the way he would teach for the kind of children he may have taught, but that it didn't work for these children. I have one student with a severe learning disability who is very non-verbal. If she comes to talk to me, am I going to make her sit down and be quiet? The way I see it is that journal time is a time for them to get their ideas generated. Some kids come in with little they can articulate, but when they hear what other kids are talking about it helps them to get writing.

I find a lot of children get stuck when they are thinking so hard about a question that they lose the connection between the question and writing. I have much better success when we talk about it before we write. I'll go up to the board and write a morning message to my class every once in a while. It's things that happened to me, and it's things that happened in the village, and I can go as far as to talk about a clan gathering that's going to be happening in the coming week. That might stimulate them, or I might talk about so and so's roof that just blew off last night, or a big cockle tide coming up, or a deer that someone just got. Then the light goes on about someone's dad also having got a deer. Even though that's my journal time, there's a lot of talking going on before the actual writing takes place.

I was kind of concerned about what my evaluation was going to look like after this discussion I had with the principal, but after it was all done and he gave it to me, it was fine. (October 1996)

Healing the community - Deborah

Right now the school district officials are trying to say that the learning is community-based, just because they've left ten copies of a planning document at the Band Office. It's important that the school become part of what's going on in the community, and gradually help to bring community people into the school. Leaving copies of a report in the Band Office isn't going to accomplish that.

As for the parents, there are quite a few who aren't involved and their kids are floundering around. It's mainly because of abuse. For me that is so hard to handle, kids coming to school with a barrel of stuff they need to get rid of. I've been trying to set up both individual and group counseling. By next September, two female counselors and myself will start some groups for girls. We'll try to do workshops on self-esteem, building it up bit by bit. I think that can work better than individual counseling.

I approached the principal, but he had a really hard time accepting it. He's afraid there's going to be an explosion. But the kids aren't learning anything because of all this emotional stuff inside of them. They don't know how to let it out, especially the girls. We are trying to figure out how we can work with the boys too. We need to find supportive leaders, young men in the community who can come and work with them. The principal said, "We don't want it to end up to be a healing place!" I thought to myself that it might have to be just that before you can get to anything else. (June 1996)

Explaining it to colleagues:
Giving voice to the echoes of the past - Marilyn

Last year we had a daily assembly where we had to bring our kids down every single day to the gym. First they had to sing this song, and then we marched them all back. There were very high expectations as to how the kids were to line up and the kids had been told these expectations. I remember the one teacher: "hips and lips!" Your hands have to be on your hips and your lips have to be closed!

When the staff met at the end of the year to discuss what to keep for the following year and the subject of assemblies came up, all the teachers said they wanted to continue them. All the teachers but me, that is. By then I knew that my job was secure, so I said that I had some objections to the assemblies. The principal asked the staff to first discuss why they wanted to continue with the assemblies. After that, one of the teachers said that she was curious to know what my objection was. I explained that marching our children up and down the hall and performing in the gym was a throwback to residential school. I said, "As a First Nations teacher, I feel that I need to help our kids get past all of that, because their parents have not been able to yet." I explained that if they chose to continue them, my class would not be participating. Mel and Bea agreed with me, and then the other teachers started to think about it.

After the meeting was over, Bea and I went back to my class, and after a few minutes there was a knock on the door. It was one of the teachers known for his strictness. He said, "I am really sorry, but I didn't realize that we were offending you this way." He then proceeded to ask us, "When I make my kids turn around and go all the way back when they are noisy, is that really bad? I mean do you see that as really bad?" He didn't realize that this was how we were seeing it. (October 1996)

IN THE PRESENT SYSTEM, WHAT IS BEST FOR THE KIDS?[57]

ELEMENTARY SCHOOL

Joe's humiliating experience

After work one day, I got a phone call from one of my friends whose nephew had had a bad experience at school that day. Her nephew's teacher had put some masking tape over the boy's mouth and left it there for about five minutes. She had done this, my friend heard, because Joe wouldn't raise his hand or keep quiet while they were reviewing something. While he had the tape on, the teacher and some of the other students were laughing at him.

Joe is in Grade 2. He is an active boy and very intelligent: not rude or disruptive. At his age, he cannot speak up for himself, and an incident like this could have a very negative effect on him. I know his parents, so I phoned and asked his dad what had happened. His dad said that they had heard about the incident from a friend's son, and that Joe had mentioned at the dinner table that he did not like what the teacher had done to him. They questioned him and found out what had happened in class.

The next day, Joe's father talked to the principal, who said he was unaware of the incident but that he would discuss it with the teacher. When the father phoned the school later, the principal assured him that he had talked to the teacher and that this would never happen again. However, the fact of the matter is that this teacher violated the Code of Ethics, and the principal didn't even know what took place. According to the Code, a teacher is not supposed to do or say anything negative to a student. This teacher had violated it on three counts: putting the tape on his mouth, leaving it there for a long period of time, and laughing at him with the other students. If the students and parents hadn't known each other, nothing at all would have been done.

---

57 In the vignettes in this section, the names of the students have been changed. The names of the narrators have been omitted in order to protect confidentiality.

I believe that all students should be allowed to feel safe and be treated with respect in the school environment. I experienced a few negative incidents going through school, and I still see and hear them taking place today. Some students and parents don't know what their rights are, or what course of action to follow when these rights are violated. Teachers who infringe on these rights should be disciplined accordingly.

Since I had only heard of the incident, I couldn't do anything directly, but I did inform the parents of the course of action they could take. I told the father that he could write to the Director of Instruction, the District Teacher's Union, and the First Nations Education Council. I recommended that he outline what had taken place in detail, and ask what course of action would be taken with the teacher. I also suggested that the parents could deal with it more directly by setting up a meeting with the teacher to hear her side of the story.

As a teacher, I am familiar with the Code of Ethics. The BC College of Teachers newsletter also outlines courses of action taken against teachers who violate this code. As a member of the First Nations Education Council, I am familiar with those in positions of power in this school district. The most difficult thing in dealing with this problem was to get the parents to go forward with it. Some First Nations parents are reluctant to assert their rights or confront people in authority.

If this were to happen again, I would go over the Teachers' Code of Ethics with the parents and answer any questions they might have about what they could do. Racism and prejudice is still present in our schools today. Parents need to take the initiative and learn how to take action. Students themselves need to know their rights. It's easy for students to lash out when faced with negative actions directed at them. They would be in a better position to deal with these situations if they knew their rights.

Sam's story

The students enrolled at the school I teach at are all First Nations. Sam is a little girl in Grade 1. She has recently missed a week of school. She arrived Monday morning with her brothers and sisters, for whom she had been babysitting for a week. Sam enjoys being at school, but she has to bring her three siblings with her if she comes.

When I see Sam I know that in the lives of some little people the kind of reinforcements we generally use in schools have no meaning. She just needs food and some hugs. She needs the primary reinforcements that satisfy a biological need: things like food, water, warmth. Secondary or conditioned reinforcements such as grades, money, and feelings of academic success have no meaning for her. Given her age and her circumstances of life, secondary reinforcement cannot reach her.

Monica's story

Our team has had a lot of problems teaching the Grade 7 Sm'algyax language class.[58] Some of the students act disrespectfully, they are rude, speak out of turn, and sometimes refuse to do what we ask. Many of them come from families where drinking, drugs, and physical or sexual abuse occur. Many of the kids are from single-parent families. Several of our Grade 7s have had in-school suspensions.

At the end of the year, during our very last language class, one of our students was saying goodbye to us, and when she hugged me I smelled what seemed to be Peach Cooler. It is an alcoholic drink that I used to drink at one time. I looked at her and she smiled. I didn't know what to do. First of all, I wasn't sure that it was alcohol I smelled. I could have been wrong. Secondly, it was the second last day of the whole school year. Last of all, I was not comfortable with the principal. She is a very strict woman who likes to run a very tight ship. I also know that

58 Participation in a second language class is mandatory for all students in B.C. beginning in Grade 5. In this school, any student can choose French or Sm'algyax.

she is prejudiced against First Nations people. I sensed this when I met her three years ago, and this is the school where I completed both of my practica.

I mentioned my concerns about Monica to my teaching partner, who is a non-drinker, but she did not smell anything on Monica. I thought for sure she had smelled it also. That sort of changed my mind about reporting it.

When I think back on this situation, I ask myself a few questions. If Monica had been drinking, was I wrong for not reporting it? What could the principal have done to her? Does Monica think that she got away with drinking at school? What message is she getting from my not reporting it? What can happen to me as a teacher in this school district for not reporting?

If I find myself in this kind of situation again, I will try to find out more details and I will document everything. Then I will consult with the principal or an administrative assistant and have them deal with it.

Julien's story

Julien is a seven-year-old First Nations boy in Grade 2, and he is new to this area. He doesn't know many of the students, and is slowly getting settled with classroom routines. However, he is struggling to understand basic concepts in spelling, math, and reading. Julien needs constant encouragement to keep "on task" and complete his work.

He often needs one-to-one instruction in math and in literacy. He benefits from working individually or in small groups each day with the learning assistance teacher. During circle time, he usually pays attention as long as he isn't within reach of another student. However, his interactions with his peers are almost always negative.

Within the first two weeks of school, I noticed how aggressive he was. I spoke to his mother, who was also concerned about his behavior. During our interview, she told me that she was struggling financially as a single mother with two children. She explained that Julien's father had been very abusive towards her, and that Julien had witnessed both verbal and physical abuse. She had sought counseling through the Ministry of Social Services, and decided to go back to a local college to complete her Grade 12. While she attends classes, her mother takes care of the two children and brings them to school.

In class and on the playground, Julien's behavior became more intolerable. In one incident, he hit a boy and the boy told me Julien did it for no reason at all. The other students confirmed this story. I asked Julien to apologize to the boy and said: "Please, do not let this happen again." Then one day Julien hit a girl in the stomach during noon hour. The lunch supervisor reported it to the principal, who suspended him for three days, and told him that he could not spend the lunch hour on the school grounds. He followed this with a letter to his mother saying that Julien's aggressive behavior would not be tolerated at school. Julien enjoys school lunches, so he felt the consequences of this being taken away from him. When he returned from the suspension he agreed not to hit anyone again. I continued to monitor his behavior.

One of the ways I deal with inappropriate behavior is to have a class meeting, where we brainstorm how to improve the behavior, and I encourage students to give examples. I then ask them to write a summary in their daily journals, and I review the list of good behaviors as often as possible. I combined this strategy with individual talks with Julien. However, aggressive incidents on the playground continued.

One day, as I was bringing the students in from recess, I saw Julien hit another student. The principal sent another letter to Julien's mother, telling her that he would be suspended from school if he continued to misbehave. Every day, I recorded Julien's aggressive behavior.

SECONDARY SCHOOL

Judy and Tom's story

In the secondary school where I teach, the majority of the students are First Nations. This story is about a boyfriend and girlfriend who attend my school. Their names are Judy and Tom.

While I was teaching a class, a student came running into my classroom and said "they are fighting again." I told the students to stay in the classroom and went to help. The principal was standing outside the girls' bathroom and he told me not to go in. I went in anyway. Tom was hanging over the bathroom stall trying to get at Judy, who had locked herself in. My instincts told me to get Tom's attention so I put myself where he could make eye contact with me. I've stopped them from fighting in the past. Tom looked at me and I could see the anger in his eyes. He said, "I'm so angry at her!" I told him that he should not touch her, even if he was angry with her. He jumped down from the stall, looked at me and ran outside. I hugged Judy and told her I was going outside to check on Tom. Again, the principal warned me that Tom might hurt me, but I didn't pay any attention. I found Tom crying outside. I held him and told him I cared for him.

Freddy talks too much

This is the second year that I have taught First Nations studies 12. The first year was exciting: it was the beginning of utilizing all my skills, knowledge, and education at the secondary level. I set out my goals, which firstly, were to offer all students an appreciation and understanding of the culture, heritage, and history of northwest coast people in British Columbia. Another goal I had was to enhance cross-cultural communication, respect, and understanding. However, the most important goal for me as an educator and as a First Nations person was to promote pride and dignity. I wanted to assist First Nations students to develop greater self-esteem and pride in their culture and heritage by learning more about their identity, history, language, and stories.

During my first year I went to work each day with ambition, energy, and enthusiasm for teaching. I spent hours setting up my curriculum. I had a diverse group of students: First Nations students from different communities, non-natives, and an exchange student from Switzerland. They were an enthusiastic group of learners able to voice their personal perspectives on issues relating to politics, the Indian Act, and band council elections. They had the ability to analyze complicated treaty processes, and developed skills in research, critical thinking, communication, and citizenship. Their behavior and attitudes were positive, and they successfully completed the course.

This year is a totally different story. While the majority of my students come with positive attitudes and are eager to learn and collaborate, I am having a major struggle with one young lad, Freddy, who persists in constantly talking in class. He is sarcastic, and continually disrupts other students so that they can't grasp the full content of what I am teaching.

One day, Freddy walked into class late and without excusing himself proceeded to his seat, disturbing others to attract attention along the way. He continued to talk in a loud, boisterous voice, making negative comments about going to school. I asked him to listen to what I was teaching about the Indian Act, and explained that learning to listen has always been one of the First Nations' primary skills. Freddy sat down, but a few minutes later he was disturbing students who were listening, and one of them began to complain that Freddy talks too much. I tried two more times to ask him to be quiet, and on the third I sent him to the principal with instructions to explain his rude behavior. Freddy left the room, but instead of going to the principal's office, he walked up and down the hallways disturbing other students. After class, I wrote up a discipline order clearly stating Freddy's negative actions and comments.

This was the beginning of my encounters with Freddy. There were several times after that that I went home with an enormous headache. I met with the school counselor to discuss different strategies I might use to change his negative attitude.

His behavior remained the same. I had to discuss his behavior with the principal, who then contacted his parents. The parents defended their son. I wished we could video their son's behavior so the parents could witness it and listen to the repulsive language he was using in school. In any event, the home contact wasn't successful, and there was very little improvement in Freddy's behavior.

Several weeks later, Freddy came in late again. He appeared to be working quietly, but in fact he was drawing and writing remarks on the table. I asked him to clean off the table, and said that I would only ask once. He didn't respond except to challenge my authority with a shrewd smile. I said in a louder and more demanding voice, "If you don't clean up the drawings, I will get the principal immediately." At this, Freddy reacted quickly and cleaned off the table.

A few weeks went by, and Freddy actually started to settle down in class. He became a bit more respectful to other students, listening to their opinions on different issues. He started to appreciate me as a First Nations teacher, recognizing my knowledge and ability to explore relevant curriculum and present a holistic perspective. Just as he was at this point, his parents pulled him out of school to work for two weeks. His parents should have been more responsible and requested his assignments in my course and others, but they didn't even inform me that he would be absent.

At the end of two quarters, Freddy barely passed the course. Freddy was indeed a challenge, but he gave me the opportunity to test my classroom management skills, challenge my level of tolerance, and learn never to take students' comments personally.

We got to know each other, and I used to tease him that I may be around long enough to teach his children. I believe I will see Freddy in another five or ten years, and perhaps he will be successful in life and a leader in his own community. I do think positively about him; that he might use his verbal skills for leadership, as an advocate for native concerns and issues. In the end, I hope I made a little difference.

Teddy's final year

Graduation is the most exciting time of the year for any Grade 12 student. It is a milestone in their lives, and a stepping-stone for those who will continue on to college or university. Every student has the opportunity to graduate, but they must make a serious commitment to accomplish this goal. They also need the support and encouragement of their parents.

Teddy has the potential and academic skills to complete all the required assignments for my Grade 12 English class, provided that he attends all classes and applies himself to completing major projects. Teddy knows he has the potential to succeed, but he chooses not to apply himself to his studies.

After the first three weeks of school, I sent home an interim progress report for English 12. I indicated Teddy's lack of attendance, and gave him and "I" designation, which means that his attendance and productivity would have to improve over the next seven weeks in order for him to pass the course. English 12 is required for graduation, so this message was particularly important. The interim was sent to Teddy's parents to ensure that they were aware of this.

At mid-term I sent another interim report to the parents indicating that Teddy had less than 50% in English 12, and reiterated that 50% was an academic requirement for graduation. I followed this with a telephone call to his mother and encouraged her to ensure that her son complete the requirements. I mentioned that I was available every day after school, and the learning assistance teacher was available every morning if he needed any further instruction or assistance with assignments. I let the principal know about the whole situation so that he could give Teddy extra encouragement or motivation to keep on task. Teddy, unfortunately, did not take these offers of support seriously.

Teddy failed at the end of the third term, and therefore was not eligible for the graduation ceremony. At the beginning of the year, Teddy and all the Grade 12 students had signed a ceremony eligibility agreement where all the requirements for participation in graduation had been clearly outlined. He had not met these requirements, and a month before the graduation ceremonies were to take place he realized he couldn't participate in them. This was devastating news for his parents and he was mortified.

Several days later, I attended the meeting with Teddy, his mother, and the school counselor. The counselor went over the agreement Teddy had signed regarding the graduation ceremonies. Because these were extra curricular activities, each student was required to participate in fund raising, and earn ten credits worth twenty dollars each. The money raised was used to pay for the prom, the casino night, dinner, and breakfast. Teddy had earned all his credits, and felt that it was grossly unfair that they would be wasted.

I presented copies of Teddy's assignments, the interim reports, a log of telephone calls, and discussions with the principal and counselor. I explained that Teddy had the ability to meet the required learning outcomes for English 12 and all other courses, and that there had been efforts to ensure that he would pass. I told them that he was not a discipline problem, that he was well mannered, that his attendance was good, and that he had the academic potential. However, because he had not made any effort to increase his mark after repeated warnings, it was now too late, and he would have to suffer the consequences. Teddy agreed that he had wasted his time, and he was now sorry for his lack of effort.

The school counselor told Teddy that he still had the potential to get his Dogwood Certificate at the end of the school year, but Teddy says that it wouldn't be the same. All his friends are graduating this year and are planning a big celebration after the ceremonies. If he were to take English 12 again next year, his friends would already be in college. He said: "I know I messed it up myself but why couldn't the teacher be a little flexible and let me finish one more assignment." I replied that I had given him sufficient time to finish his required assignments, that he had had three interim reports, and that now it was too late.

As an educator from a First Nations background, I cannot favor one First Nations student and pass him when he has not successfully completed the requirements for the course. In my opinion, it is unprofessional and unethical to pass a student who has not met the learning outcomes, especially when the student has been given plenty of opportunities.

Eddie's struggles

Eddie has just moved from a small village school with a familiar and safe environment to an urban centre in order to complete his secondary education, because Grades 11 and 12 are not available in his home community. His parents were separated when he was very young, and he has lived with his extended family of aunts and grandparents. Eddie's grandparents love him and cater to his every whim. His immediate family members call him a spoiled kid.

Eddie is the youngest student in my class, and is constantly struggling with meeting the objectives of the Grade 12 curriculum. His attendance is perfect, and he is always on time. He gets a monthly education allowance from his band based on attendance. If he misses a class, a part of it is deducted, so it is quite a strong motivator for him to attend. Not all First Nations students receive an allowance, and this sometimes becomes a serious issue. Other students feel left out when they see the home-school coordinator handing out cheques, and wonder why they don't have the same privilege. It is only available for those students who have to relocate because they do not offer the appropriate grade levels in their village.

Eddie has made the transition to a large urban secondary school fairly well, but he tends to be sarcastic to other students. He laughs at other students who make an effort to answer questions. He has no problem with oral presentations or quizzes, but he finds it extremely difficult to write exams. When he doesn't understand the content or when the work becomes too challenging, he rebels. He becomes very distracted, will not accept my instruction, and makes excuses for not completing assignments. When I ask him a question that he cannot respond to, he just shrugs his shoulders or makes comments that are irrelevant to what we are doing. If I ask him to tell me what he doesn't understand, rather than shrugging his shoulders, he continues to say, "I don't know." On a few occasions, when I asked him a question and I saw that he was embarrassed because of his lack of comprehension, I asked another student to explain the question in order to draw attention away from him.

After continuing negative conduct and successive phone calls to his home, I had to give him an "I" for incomplete. It is school policy for students to be put on probation if they fail two or more courses. Eddie was put on probation in the first and second quarters, and again in the third, when he failed more than four courses. A meeting was called to discuss Eddie's future education with his guardians, home-school coordinator, counselor, and special needs counselor. When I reviewed his files to prepare for the meeting, I discovered that in Grade 7 he was already performing more than two years behind in math, language arts, and social studies and that he was placed on a modified language arts and science program for Grades 7, 8, and 9. His attitude and behavior were documented as unsatisfactory.

After reviewing his records, I came to the conclusion that he should have remained in a modified program and not been forced into the mainstream academic system until he could comprehend the basics necessary for success. In my opinion, his hostile behavior was the result of not understanding how to read the content of Grade 12 courses. He was probably trying to cover up his inability to read or comprehend by acting out.

At the meeting, the special consultant presented the assessment that indicated that Eddie's reading and comprehension was at a very low level. His auntie said that she felt Eddie should be in a modified program, but his grandfather disagreed. His expectations for his grandson are very high, and he believed Eddie would change. After a lengthy discussion, it was agreed that Eddie would remain in the regular program with weekly monitoring.

Eddie remained on probation, and in the third term he passed PE and failed the other four courses. I believe he is just being pushed through the system and becoming more angry and frustrated because he can't understand the content of his grade level.

Similar situations occur for many First Nations students who are struggling to understand the academic content. However, school policy states that any students failing two or more courses during four quarters should be referred to the alternate school. Perhaps Eddie's grandfather will agree to put him in a modified program if, at the end of this quarter, he is referred to the alternate school.

TEACHER AS PARENT

That TOC

My daughter Cheryl is in Grade 7. Recently, their class had a teacher-on-call for a few days. I heard from another teacher-on-call that she had seen my daughter sitting outside the classroom on a bench. She heard the substitute teacher come out of the class and talk very loudly while pointing her finger in my daughter's face. When I asked Cheryl what had happened, she said that the teacher had called her immature, and said that she had acted like a four-year-old. She told her that she liked being the centre of attention and whined when she wasn't. I asked my daughter what had brought this on, and she said that the teacher liked using her and her class group as an example to the rest of the class.

I could not believe this. Cheryl has a very quiet and shy nature. She has never gotten in trouble like this. She has been in a gifted program since Grade 4. I went to the principal, who I have known since my daughter started Grade 1. He agreed to talk to the teacher, and she said she would not do this again. I was still very upset, because according to my friend, the teacher-on-call was being abusive to my child, pointing a finger in her face and screaming negative remarks at her. I set up a meeting with the teacher for after school, but when I arrived she had already left. I went to the principal again, but he said he couldn't really do anything about it, because it was the second to last day of the school year.

I was angry about the whole incident. No teacher has the right to humiliate and abuse children. She had violated the teachers' Code of Ethics and gotten away with it. I might never have known what took place if it had not been for my friend who was a teacher-on-call in that school. I thought that knowing the principal would benefit me. However, in my opinion, he did not deal with the situation properly. The fact that it was so close to the end on school really hindered me. If it had been a week earlier, I would have demanded further action. As a new teacher-on-call myself, I also felt vulnerable.

If this were to happen again I would have a better idea how to deal with it. I would insist on meeting with the teacher because it's necessary to know both sides of the story. If I wasn't happy with the outcome, I would pursue it by writing a letter to the director of instruction with copies to the District Teachers' Union and the First Nations Education Council. I would contact them to see how the situation was dealt with. It could even be pursued through the B.C. College of Teachers.

Clayton's story

For seven years I sent my son Clayton off to be part of a school system where he felt that he was a stupid person. During that time, he would come home and say that he wished he were dead. School was an extremely frustrating experience for him. Finally, we pulled him out and set him up to learn at home with computer-assisted instruction (CAT). He has been on e-bussing for two years now, and is an example of the success of using computers for schooling. CAT is frequently shown to be superior to traditional instruction in terms of both increasing academic achievement and improving students' attitudes towards schoolwork. Clayton has accomplished a great deal in the past two years, and working with computers has given him an opportunity to develop the skill of how to work by himself.

Clayton's situation has caused me to ask some bigger questions about First Nations students within the school system. Are all First Nations students put into learning assistance simply because they are First Nations students? Can we help teachers see our students with different eyes? Can we help to change the school system?

SUGGESTED DISCUSSION QUESTIONS

1. How can new teachers who feel vulnerable assert themselves when they feel that rules and conventional ways for doing things in school don't help the learners?

2. What discourses are in conflict when you are both a teacher and a trusted community member in whom parents confide about problems with teachers and schools? Is it possible to respect both professional and community expectations?

3. What historical discourses make it difficult for parents to develop the power to voice their questions and ask for their rights? What can teachers do to help them?

4. What are the responsibilities of a teacher and community regarding students who have needs for protection?

5. Consider the actions you have taken when you found yourself in a situation that you see as unjust or unethical. What aspects of your responses feel positive and effective to you? What do you wish you could do more effectively? What steps might you take to improve your effectiveness?

6. What have you observed are the reasons that so many First Nations children are put in learning assistance from an early age? How do discourses of "failure" and "under-achievement" misrepresent students' abilities? Are there other discourses and related practices that might be more helpful? What alternative models based on Indigenous educational discourses might be more useful and appropriate? Does your district collect statistical information on the percentages of First Nations learners who are labeled as "learning disabled" or other special designations?

7. What practices are in place in your school for students who are failing? How do these practices position the students, and how do they position you? Do they help the student to make positive changes? Do they benefit the other students in the class? Are there other practices and discourses that would be more inclusive? How can "alternate" programs avoid or resist stigmatization? How might you draw on Indigenous pedagogical approaches in responding to these issues?

8. In issues of classroom management, when is it beneficial to make exceptions for students with difficult circumstances? When is it important to enforce consequences? What are the similarities between normative school discourses of classroom management, and community-based Indigenous discourses on education? What are the differences? What possible ways might these two discourses be negotiated or bridged?

9. When students arrive in secondary school, they may have already experienced years of schooling that can deplete their sense of strong First Nations identity. What does this tell you about the struggles they may carry into secondary schools, even when their teachers are First Nations teachers committed to their well-being?

10. Who do you think can benefit from home schooling? In what cases as a teacher might you recommend it to a parent?

11. What discourses are in conflict when you are both a teacher and a parent with a child in a colleague's classroom? How might you present your predicament to a colleague in ways that would win their support, rather than making them feel that you are judging their professional practice?

CHAPTER 9:
ARTICULATING NEW
APPROACHES FOR SCHOOLS

This district is really, really busy in terms of First Nations educational programs. When we get together with other districts and talk about all the things that we do, they said "Oh my God. We want your money. Where are you guys getting your money? Why do you get all this stuff?" And we said, "You know what? You do get our money, you do get targeted funds, and you could do this if there were people in control of it like the First Nations Education Council here in Prince Rupert." That is just the way it is.

(Marilyn)

In the same way that Marilyn asserts the importance of being "in control," contemporary scholars of Indigenous pedagogy Menzies, Q'um Q'um xiiem, Archibald & Hingaroa Smith, specify "the need to be positive and proactive in developing transformation for themselves" (2004, p. 1). In Prince Rupert, this work was initiated by the North Coast Tribal Council. The First Nations Education Council now has responsibility for this advocacy work. (First Nations Education Council, 2005)[59]

This chapter outlines the formal activities of the Sm'algyax language and Ts'msyen culture programs. Informal community social practices and the ways they are integrated in classrooms are also described. These social practices include approaches for teaching about the difficult history of residential schooling. Finally, English literacy programming, which builds on Indigenous pedagogical approaches to building communication between school and community are illustrated.

The initiatives for a Sm'algyax language program, Ts'msyen curriculum resource development, and the personnel needed

59 The First Nations Education Council allocates funds that are designated and targeted by the Ministry of Education to provide programs and services to First Nations learners

to create and implement these programs began in the late 1970s and early 1980s. The subsequent creation in 1989 of the district First Nations Education Council established a formal structure for their ongoing development and implementation, and is reinforced by the Partnership Agreement between the council and the school district (2005). Another major collaborative initiative of the school district and the council is the English literacy program.

The teachers who contributed to this book are involved in a variety of ways with each of the programs outlined below. The vignettes in this chapter illustrate the centrality of language, dance, oral narrative, and participation of all ages and diverse skills in First Nations community activities. They also illuminate how incorporating Indigenous social practices of care for all persons, respect for life, generosity, and holistic approaches enliven learning for students and their families. These approaches all help to create a cultural world where students and parents can creatively construct their identities.

SM'ALGYAX LANGUAGE AND TS'MSYEN CULTURE

The Sm'algyax language program is at the heart of reconfigured educational programming, and a variety of avenues for accessing Ts'msyen culture radiate from it. Sm'algyax language learning, and creating a print form for a language that was traditionally not written are vital to the ongoing process of building community.[60] These programs illustrate and support theories about the pivotal role that print media can play in how people construct a sense of community (Anderson, 1983).

---

60 In the vignette "A glimpse into the Sm'algyax language program", Isabelle notes that the students in her classes are connected to a range of languages spoken in the Ts'msyen territory, i.e., Sm'algyax, Nisga'a, Gitxsan, Haisla. These were important in trade, winter ceremonial potlatches, and in marriage. It is customary to use the language of the region in which you are living. Many of the elders in the region are conversant in a number of these languages. Other school districts in Ts'msyen territory have parallel developments in language programming in their local languages.

In *Imagined Communities,* Anderson (1983) draws extensively on historical examples from Indonesia, Europe, and South America to illustrate how colonial governments used literacy as a tool to impose conformity to a single government. Anderson's description is reminiscent of how the Canadian government, working through the churches and public schools, sought to subjugate Aboriginal communities through the use of national languages (English and French).

The Sm'algya̱x language and Ts'msyen culture programs described here work on building the Ts'msyen nation, but do so with the intent of stimulating identification rather than enforcing control. Outlined below is an overview of the personnel who develop, implement, and monitor these programs. This is followed by itemizations of the print and web-based resources, activity-based curriculum, and the connections among these.

PERSONNEL

Since the early 1970s, elders have taught Sm'algya̱x in village schools on a daily basis. Beginning in the mid-1970s, there was also a paraprofessional training program to assist the elders in their classroom work. Using their work as a foundation, the Northcoast Tribal Council employed linguists[61] to work collaboratively with fluent speakers of the local languages. Together they compiled grammars and dictionaries and transcribed a considerable number of *adawx* (historical narratives, or "true tellings") that are the core of the current print and web-based resources.

First Nations and some non-First Nations teachers – as well as First Nations resource people – were hired to create and publish a series of bilingual guides to the history and culture

----

61   The following linguists have worked in a variety of ways to assist in the development of language programming over the last 20 years: Jean Mulder, John Dunn, Chuck Natkong, and Marianne Boelscher-Ignace.

of the region in 1992.[62] Working collaboratively with elders, and with the support of the First Nations Education Council and First Nations Education Services of the Prince Rupert District, First Nations teachers and resource people have now published more than forty books on a variety of aspects of history, culture, and language (Appendix 5).[63] Local artists professionally illustrated many of these materials. Students and teachers in villages created some of the resources (Hartley Bay School, 1996, 1997).

The innovative programming in Sm'algyax language initiated in the 1980s is continuously enhanced with new resources. There are currently six full-time Sm'algyax teachers (with provincial teaching certification) who work collaboratively with five fully fluent speakers to provide language classes in all schools in the district. As well, they work with classroom teachers on developing strategies for integrating Sm'algyax language and Ts'msyen culture into the mainstream curriculum. Several First Nations educators in Prince Rupert who worked on these curriculum projects also worked on a Ministry of Education curriculum committee to develop a province-wide First Nations studies curriculum and textbook for Grade 12 (Campbell, Menzies & Peacock, 2003). Teachers' creativity in bringing in their own personal knowledge and experiences enhance these formal materials.

---

62 Some of these materials were adapted from *adawx* originally transcribed in Sm'algyax and English by William Beynon between 1914 and 1954, transcribed in current orthography by John Dunn (1991), edited by Pauline Dudoward, John Dunn, Verna Helin, Vonnie Hutchingson, Susan Marsden, Beatrice Robinson, Marie-Louise Tarpent, and Mildred Wilson. Drafts of the works-in-progress were submitted to thirty-one Ts'msyen elders from four different villages for consultation and commentary.

63 The First Nations Resource Catalogue lists 43 resources that can be ordered from First Nations Education Services. All materials were developed by First Nations Education Services under the direction of the First Nations Education Council and School District #52 (Prince Rupert) at 317 9th Avenue West, Prince Rupert, BC V8J 2S6. Phone 250-627-1536; fax 250-627-1443; www.sd52.bc.ca/fnes/

The teacher education students enrolled in three successive offerings of the SFU teacher education program, and had a wide variety of backgrounds and levels of fluency in Sm'algya̱x. Some of these individuals are now sufficiently skilled to work alongside fluent elders developing and teaching the language curriculum.[64] Since the late 1980s, the First Nations Education Council has successfully advocated for district staff specialist positions to coordinate First Nations language and culture programming. At present, there are four full-time positions: the First Nations department head, a curriculum developer, the First Nations literacy resource teacher, and a First Nations education program resource teacher, all of whom are committed to full-time work expanding, implementing, and monitoring programs. Three full-time family resource workers support their work.[65]

PRINT AND WEB-BASED APPROACHES

The description of personnel makes it apparent that the work in the language and culture programs is not easily separated. The two areas of overlap, and are mutually supportive. This is also visible in the following catalogue of approaches.

• The Sm'algya̱x Language Program, approved by the B.C. Ministry of Education, is available in all district schools. In Prince Rupert, it begins in Grade 5. In the village schools, it starts in kindergarten. On the website *www.sd52.bc.ca/fnes/online.html*,

---

64 At many points in the five-year teacher education program, the participants stressed their hopes that through participation in this program they would become fluent speakers. While several courses were offered in Sm'algya̱x language, many of the participants found this was not sufficient for them to attain the levels of fluency they desired. Ongoing university-sponsored language courses are now offered by the University of Northern BC and Northwest Community College, and the language teachers have enrolled in these.

65 Local First Nations educators, including Kathy Bedard, Marilyn Bryant, Vonnie Hutchingson, Debbie Jeffrey, Debbie Leighton-Stephens, and have filled the majority of the positions coordinating the language and culture programs. Some of the teachers involved in these programs, as well as in classroom teaching positions, are graduates of the University of British Columbia.

you can hear place name pronunciations. Vocabulary for the curriculum unit entitled *Honouring the Salmon* is available at *www.sd52.bc.ca/fnes/sf2.html.*

• Ts'msyen curriculum resources support the mandatory use of Ts'msyen cross-curricular theme units from Grades 1 to 7 (see list and order form of supporting resources in Appendix 2). A multimedia site on precontact life called *Connecting Traditions* is available at *www.sd52.bc.ca/fnes/tsimshian/ct.html.* The most recent resource, *Persistence and Change: A History of the Ts'msyen Nation* (Campbell, 2005) is a richly illustrated text that supports the B.C. provincial First Nations Studies 12 curriculum, as well as serving as a resource for other grade levels. A seven-unit secondary school science and social studies curriculum: *Forests and Oceans for the Future* emphasizes traditional ecological knowledge. The units can be downloaded from the website *www.ecoknow.ca/curriculum.html.*[66]

• First Nations Library. This collection is held at the District Resource Centre for the use of all teachers.

ACTIVITY-CENTRED APPROACHES

• First Nations Role Model Program. Supporting the curriculum development initiatives, The Role Model Program is a network of local First Nations artists, dancers, musicians and other skilled community members who are remunerated by the school district to serve as resource people for school and classroom programs. Any teacher in the district can request role models to engage students in activities in a wide variety of areas, including story telling, carving, painting drumming, dancing and singing. Classroom visits by role models provide

66 The unit "Traditional Plant Knowledge of the Tsimshian" is used in the new Grade 12 program in Hartley Bay. The author Judy Thompson, whose ancestry is Tahltan, is a former student of the Simon Fraser Teacher Education Program. She is on faculty at the University of Northern British Columbia. In Thompson, 2004 she documents the methodological and pedagogical background to her work on this unit.

an opportunity for classes not taught by First Nations teachers to have experiences with First Nations adults with a wide range of skills. These visits also provide back up and support for the First Nations classroom teachers. A visible symbol of their importance is a series of poster-size full color photographs of the role models, which are widely displayed in a variety of educational and community settings.

• First Nations Elementary Program. This program, enrolling fifteen to twenty Grade 5/6 students (per year), is intended for students considered "at risk" for leaving school. It integrates considerable First Nations content and activities with the B.C. curriculum.

• National Aboriginal Day Celebration (June 21). This district-wide event features activities and performances based on four principles of relationships between Aboriginal people and Canada, outlined by the Royal Commission on Aboriginal Peoples: mutual recognition, respect, sharing, and responsibility. A performance by internationally acclaimed Inuit vocalist Susan Aglukark recently featured.

The first three vignettes in this chapter illustrate how teachers integrated Sm'algyax language and Ts'msyen cultural activities on a daily basis. Vignettes illustrating how teachers knowledgeable in Ts'msyen culture and Sm'algyax language continuously infuse their personal knowledge and identities into their work follow.

LANGUAGE AND CULTURE

A glimpse into the Sm'algyax language program - Isabelle

I am working on my ninth year teaching the Sm'algyax (Ts'msyen dialect) language. I work with a fluent speaker. Over the years, I have learned so much. It is good for the students to see me as a learner as well. I teach Grade 5, 6, and 7 students from all backgrounds. There are Ts'msyen, Nisga'a, Haida, Gitxsan, Haisla, Métis, and non-native students.

We use the International Phonetic Alphabet to record the Sm'algyax dialect. I will use some words in my examples. The fonts we use are the Sm'algyax serif and Sm'algyax sans. These fonts can be downloaded from the internet onto your computer. (*http://www.sd52.bc.ca/fnes/fonts.html*)

At the beginning of the year, we teach the students to introduce themselves by name, crest, where they are from, and where they live. The fluent speaker and I model each question and answer. The students work in pairs, and practice until they are confident enough to introduce themselves to one another. When they have mastered this, we model introducing another person. The endings change. Take for example, the root word *waa*. It means "name". *Waayu* means "name (my)". *Waat* means "name (her/his)".

The Sm'algyax teachers were having supper at a local restaurant one Friday afternoon after a long day of working on curriculum. One of our students from Conrad Elementary School came in with his family. I couldn't remember his name. After awhile, I went over to his table and asked *Naayu di waan*?

(What is your name?) Without hesitation, he answered *Brayden di waayu*. We were pretty pleased with his ability to answer our questions.

We teach the students how to refer to immediate family members. We do this by using family photographs, modeling, and playing games. I will point to a picture of my mother and say *Nooyu gwa'a*. The actual translation is "Mother (my) this is." *Mabel di waat* ("Mabel is name [her]"). We go around the room and say, "This is my father, his name is...." If it is a possibility, the students answer *oo* for yes, or *ayn* for no. We try to trick them when they get pretty good at the terms for family members. I will go to a male student and say *Nooyu gwa'a . . . oo ligi ayn*? ("This is my mother... yes or no?") The students think this is pretty funny. It is something that they will remember!

I happened to meet a Grade 6 Nisga'a student in the shopping mall. He was with his mom, dad, and baby sister. In Sm'algyax, I asked him who they were. He was able to answer me correctly. He used all the right terms easily.

Nooyu gwa'a. ("This is my mother.") *Margaret di waat.* ("Her name is Margaret.") *Nagwaadu gwa'a.* ("This is my dad.") *Wesley di waat.* ("His name is Wesley.")

Some terms are complicated. A boy calls his brother *wek.* A girl calls her sister *lgaawk.* The term for brother-to-sister and sister-to-brother is *lmkdii.* He said, "*lmkdyu gwa'a Danielle di waat.*" ("This is my sister. Her name is Danielle.") I was very proud of him, and told his family so!

Students also learn greetings. We do not have one word for hello. We say "*Ndaayu wila waan*" ("How are you feeling?") Students answer "*Luk'wil aam wila waalu*" (I am feeling really good) or "*Akadi aam wila waalu*" ("I am not feeling good"). There are several students, especially those in Grade 5, who will ask us this question when they see us anywhere. They will wait for us to add "*Dis' nüün?*" ("And you?").

Last year we worked on a play called *Txeemsm and the Children.* The students painted a beautiful backdrop showing the edge of a village. We condensed the play to eleven lines. Each student had a line to say (in Sm'algyax) and act out. There was no need for translation. This year, many students told us that they still remember their line. They wanted to do it again. We are working on a romantic play about a Haida chief who built an island for a Kitkatla princess.

Before Christmas we taught students Christmas carols in Sm'algyax. It was up to them how many they wanted to learn. Our students at Seal Cove Elementary School learned three songs: "O Christmas Tree," "Up On The Rooftop" and "Jingle Bells." They sang them very well at the Christmas concert. One of my Gitxsan cousins sang all three songs to her grandmother. Her grandmother was so happy, she just cried!

We give the students short little assignments to do at home. For clothing items, they write down the color of the clothes that they are wearing. (The Sm'algyax equivalent of "wearing" is "using"). They need to take this home and read it to someone and have that person initial it. For example: "*Hooyu gwisgwasgm p'axs, masgm kslüüsk ada t'u'utsgm ts'ooxsahałoo*" ("I am using blue pants, a red shirt, and black running shoes").

We gave the students a quiz on twelve of the most popular foods that they like (traditional and non-traditional). Most of them got twelve out of twelve. Students took their marked quizzes home and read it to someone, and had that person initial it. They are able to tell us in Sm'algyax what foods they like and dislike.

Right now, students are writing booklets in Sm'algyax entitled *We are going to eat*. Each student writes out the following in Sm'algyax, and then fills in the blanks with their own choices of foods. For example:

1) My father fried _____ and _____.
2) My mother boiled _____and_____; and baked _____.
3) I made _____ and fixed a drink of _____.
4) My brother/sister put the dishes, forks, cups, sugar, salt and pepper on the table.
5) We all sat around the table. My grandpa/grandma/aunt/uncle/etc. prayed. We all ate heartily.
6) Mmmm! The food we ate was delicious!

Each of the above items is on a separate page of the booklet, and the students illustrate each page. When the booklets are finished, the students' homework is to take their booklet home and read it to someone in their family. Ninety-eight percent of our students make it a point to complete their homework. The students are thoroughly enjoying this activity.

We adapt a lot of games in order for the students to remember the words, phrases, questions, and answers. We play a Sm'algyax version of tic tac toe, hangman, jeopardy, around the world, quiet ball, red rover, and bingo.

We are becoming more visible around the schools and in the community. We are putting Sm'algyax signs up for each teacher's classroom. *Suwilaay'msgm* Ms. Gibson. (Teacher, Ms. Gibson.) The library is *wåp liitsx* (house for reading). The washroom is *ts'uusgm ts'a waabu* (small house). We have Sm'algyax terms for the girls' bathroom, the boys' bathroom, the computer room, the staff room, the gymnasium, the playground, door, window, desk, blackboard, table, chair, floor, and pen, pencil, eraser, ruler, notebook, etc.

I have just started up my dance group again. I have not done it for a couple of years, since my dad passed away. Now I feel ready to pursue it again. It is hard, getting people out. Many are hesitant because they think they do not know the language well enough. I encourage them by telling them that it is so easy to learn to sing with the big song charts that I have. Some prefer just to drum, which is fine. Others are afraid that they are not dancing correctly. I tell them that there is not one right way to dance. You can be very creative in your dance moves. I will take these songs into the classroom to show students how easy it is to learn and have fun at the same time.

The fluent speakers in and out of the school system have always been a tremendous support system for me. One challenge is getting more people interested. Finding creative ways to present the material is fun. More people are showing interest.

(April 2006)

Sharing stories and songs - Pansy and Bea

I am currently writing a story about the Golden Spruce that my grandmother told me when I was quite young. My mother has also added pieces to this story. It is one in a collection called *Haida Eagle Treasure*. I chose that title for the collection because I am from the Eagle clan. I have told this story to my primary classes as my morning opening. It is a story about how a boy didn't listen to his grandfather. The moral of the story is how to listen. These little kids are so honest. They are very serious about the story.

I also read them my story about how I use Indian medicines. Then they told me about the medicines that their grandparents use. Their observations as tiny little primary kids are so interesting. When I read them my stories, they reflect back to their own personal background, which is neat. They tell me that their grandparents use grease [oolichan oil] for a bad cold. Sometimes they tell me things about the way their Ts'msyen grandparents prepare grease. The students always listen to everyone else, and they are curious and ask questions. After a story, I always ask if any one has any questions or comments, or maybe they have stories that they want to tell.

One day a student told a story about when he was walking to school and saw a little deer prancing. That is how he described how the deer was running: he said it was "prancing and dancing", so he was really using his imagination. The parents get really excited when I tell them about the imaginative things that their children do with their stories.

I have also asked Isabelle (working through the district Role Model Program) to come to the class and read stories in Sm'algyax. She has read three different stories so far from the resource collection. These books are written in English and Sm'algyax. First she reads it in English, and then in Sm'algyax. I have also done stories that the students illustrated with their own drawings and with photos that we took in the community. We put the pictures in a "big book" format.

When Isabelle sang songs with the students, she sang the songs in Sm'algyax. The rhythm and repetition of the songs make it easier to learn in Sm'algyax. Isabelle taught them two Sm'algyax songs, and I taught them two Haida songs. They really enjoy singing these, and learn them very quickly. They were able to sing these songs for the rest of the school when we did our school-wide banners project. (Pansy, October 2005)

I've included Sm'algyax songs and stories in my class. There are some songs like "The Welcome" and "The Four Crests" that are songs that anyone can sing. I have also brought in a wonderful *adawx* about the beaver and the porcupine. I have used this in a number of grade levels, and was recorded on tape by Ernie Hill, the principal over in Hartley Bay. Beaver and porcupine used to be very good friends until they played mean tricks on each other, and it wrecked their friendship forever. The theme of friendship, what it is, and what could happen if it is not nurtured stands out for me. I think this is so important for the kids. In my Grade 3/4 class we made dioramas illustrating the stories, and we displayed them all in the library.

What I remember very clearly about this is the effect it had on one boy in my class who is bright and street smart. He never finished his work, but for this project he was one of the first kids finished. I had to praise him up and down because he cut out the wings of a bird and a little beak. It was so wonderful. He had every detail, and it was amazing how fast he did it. I had had him in Grade 1 and I had never seen him do anything artistic before, but hook him into that story and get him interested in the language and it just got him going.

I had some kids from other classes who came to my class to work on this project, and I had them coming up to me in the hall "do we get to go to your class again this week; do we get to go back and do our dioramas?" It is really cool when those kids ask me. It inspires me to be a little bit more creative, and thinking how else can I keep this feeling going? I would like to bring in one of the role models, do another song. I would love to do a mask. I did a mask program at another school when I worked with the district elementary program for First Nations students at Seal Cove Elementary. I also did a traditional tool-making project with them. I know I was very artistic in high school, and it kind of brings back the artistic feeling that I had. (Bea, December 2005)

Sm'algy_ax for all the grades - Bea

Presently, we don't have Sm'algy_ax in the schools in the city of Prince Rupert until Grade 5. That is because provincial requirements specify that French or some other second language instruction is mandatory, starting in Grade 5. But at the Cedar Road preschool (Aboriginal Head Start, not part of the public school system) they are doing it with much younger children. I totally agree with the principal of Roosevelt, who wants to bring the language program in for the preschool Hub program, because the kids will be taking Sm'algy_ax in Grade 4 or 5. Why not start sooner? They are so shy by intermediate grades. In kindergarten, you give them a month and they are all yapping. We sing a song in English, then I do my Sm'algy_ax version, and they learn it. We all have fun with it. They are more comfortable with themselves as kindergarten children than when they are in Grade 5. They laugh and giggle. I would really like to add something in counting, but we will just do the basic numbers.

In Sm'algyax there are several ways of counting. Six of these are used in the new Ts'msyen calendar. There is an abstract way; counting fish or animals is done differently. Counting inanimate objects (e.g., boats) and counting humans is different yet again; and humans are counted in yet another way if they are in a boat. Right now they are just teaching the abstract in the schools. This is all very complicated, and for the work on the new calendar the entire language team (teachers, resource developers, elders, and the fluent speakers) had to get together and make sure they all agree on how to present this numbering system and how to illustrate it with pictures to make it clear for the students.

They have created a combination of pictures and charts that illustrates six ways of counting. For example, in the picture for the number one there is one seagull sitting on a log, but there are several boats tied up behind it. Then there is a chart along the bottom where you can look up the number six under the heading animals, or look up the number eight under the heading boats. This is very hard; it is complicated and time-consuming work.[67]

No matter what I am teaching,
I teach the First Nations language and culture - Isabelle

First Nations teachers are under-represented in schools. Almost 50% of the children here are First Nations and yet there are only about 2% of the teachers who are. A First Nations teacher represents these children, as well as keeping everyone's best interest in mind. A First Nations teacher is a local historian who can help them understand their true history that they don't see in textbooks. That's true for non-First Nations children as well. Everyone should know the true history of the area they're living in. Just as we are learning to live with the non-native,

---

67 For an example of a game that helps students to learn these different numbering systems, go to *www.sd52.bc.ca/fnes/tsimshian/tsim_index.html*.

the non-native should really understand and have a chance to see First Nations teachers and other professionals in their working capacities. It is so important to have a lot of cross-cultural experiences, and it is a learning experience in itself to have a First Nations teacher.

In my line of teaching, I teach the language and culture no matter what I'm teaching. It's a bit harder in subjects like science: I have to do a bit more research on plants and animals. I don't really do it in math, but with the rest I can bring in the language and first-hand cultural experiences. For the non-native kids, it is also neat. They pick up on the pronunciation just as well as everyone else. There's no difference; in fact, they're sometimes better. I don't know if I could teach any other way. There would always have to be a bit of the language and culture in there.

I think the students tend to remember a First Nations teacher more. I still have students saying "hi" to me that I taught two years ago when I just went in as a First Nations role model. I think it's an advantage, because you're sort of in the limelight and they remember what you did. It's novel to them. Another important factor is that everyone knows you. I went into another class where I know three-quarters of the kids, and I had been warned that there were supposed to be three problem boys in the class. I actually never did figure out who they were. They know you, and they are interested in what you have to say and how you present it. I always make connections to the child's experience back home: what's relevant to them, what their everyday life is like. I always look for extensions for what's in the curriculum guides. That's the advantage First Nations teachers have. I see myself as someone who can make school relevant, make it an exciting place to learn. I feel comfortable in the class, and I guess the kids sense it.

It is the community as a whole that says what is going to be taught. This city is a really unique place because we now have 35% to 40% permanent First Nations residents.[68] That wasn't the case before 1980. We're having more of a say in developing

68 Presently, due to overall declining enrollments in the district, this has risen to 50%.

curriculum and getting more activities and materials into the classroom that weren't there before. It is going to be interesting to watch what happens over the next two years in this city that only had two First Nations teachers and now has ten more. We are not all going to be teaching in the city, but the percentage of First Nations teachers has shot up. Having all these teachers in the community will definitely have an impact on the curriculum.

It is really important to know our political boundaries and make sure that parents know everything you are teaching. We also need to be very aware of political action behind the scenes. We'd be lost if we didn't have a sense of that. Politics plays a big role in our lives as teachers, and we have to be aware of everything that affects our presence in the classroom. Sometimes there are issues that are really important, and other times we don't really have to worry about it, but we always need to be aware of the issues. This is true not only in our own community, but in other communities as well. You learn from what's happened in other communities. (1995)

Visual Arts: The Banners Project - Pansy

All of the children at Conrad Street School (First Nations and non-First Nations) participated in making four large banners representing four major clan crests in this region: eagle, raven, killer whale, and wolf. These banners can be seen on the school district Internet site.[69] All of the K to 7 teachers used this project as a component in their First Nations studies program. For two and a half months, three students from each class came into my classroom for half an hour at a time to participate in drawing, tracing designs, cutting fabric and sewing buttons. They kept rotating through until every student participated in tracing, drawing, and cutting. It was an awesome project. Each student felt validated that they were making a contribution to a banner and learning the significance and meaning of the designs.

---

69 *www.sd52.bc.ca/photo/please_rename_me*. For enlargements click on slide show.

On the last day of school we had a ceremony, and two Ts'msyen elders came in with regalia. We selected four students from different classes to carry in each banner, and one Sm'algyax teacher came and explained the meaning of each crest. I also had one of the volunteers from the First Nations Role Model Program come in for twelve visits to help me out, because I couldn't teach my class and keep this project going at the same time. One of the classroom support workers worked with the role model. I did the actual instruction and explanation, and then I let them carry on. It worked out just great.

There was district support because they were willing to come up with the resources to have all those helpers. It was a school-based decision to use the resources in the way we did. The principal provided most of the necessary materials, and there was great team-work from all the teachers who sent groups of kids to my classroom. I donated all the pearl buttons; I bought them wholesale in Vancouver, but they are expensive. I could have probably done fundraising, but I didn't have the time to try and get other funding, so I just decided I'd donate all the buttons myself. I didn't have enough time to get all the fundraising done. All the buttons had to be sewn on by hand. It is a great deal of work.

My brother did two of the designs, and then I used the Ts'msyen coloring book for the wolf and the killer whale designs. I taught the students the Ts'msyen and Haida words for all of the crests. The kids were very excited about the project and the banners are now hanging in the Conrad School gym.

I also did a project like this at the Friendship House when I was teaching adults. We did one large banner containing all four of the crests. It was the biggest banner you ever could see, and all of my students worked on the banner. (October 2005)

Name giving ceremonies - Marilyn

There was feast in Port Simpson one year. It was very big, and we spent a lot of time in our Grade 4/5 class talking about it, leading up to it, what was going to happen, and I did have people come into my class and talk about it, and then after the feast we talked about what we learned about it and then what we saw.

It was a name-giving feast; they gave 143 names. They also did a pole-raising of quite an old pole, and then they gave out all the names. In Ts'msyen, when your baby is born you give them a name, and some people will say the name and blow into the baby's mouth and that is putting the name, that is who the baby is going to be. When the baby gets older, they get a child's name, and then when they become a woman they get a woman's name, and – depending on the rank in their tribe – they may get a name indicating rank. My mother-in-law got a high-ranking name, and there is one above her, and so she is now going to take the one above her and that means she is the matriarch.

My husband was given a name, and now he is going to be given another name, and he is going to have a house, he is going to be a house leader. He is going to have people below him in rank. There are different house leaders, and then there is the chief. You need to be worthy of receiving a name like that, because it is a lot of responsibility. If you are a house leader, you need to be aware of what is happening in your house, and the kinship relationships among the members of the house. You have to have good knowledge of your culture.

In my class alone, there were two boys and a girl who got names. It was pretty amazing, because a lot of kids in the school got names at the same time. They were children's names. All the kids, in my class and other classes, were really anxious to tell their names. All the teachers were saying "Oh, so-and-so is getting this name and they are all excited." The kids were finding out what their names mean. There is always a meaning to the name. It was really interesting. There is supposed to be another feast in the spring, and preparations are starting now.

We are starting to collect the gifts that will be given. It is going to be interesting.

Meetings and discussion were held for more than a year in the village to plan the name giving. Names were being lost. There were names that were dormant for years that no one had passed on. When it came to treaty negotiations, community members were noticing that other villages and other nations, like the Nisga'a, knew their history, just like that, and they knew where their names came from. They knew who a name belonged to. I think that in Port Simpson (Lax Lgu'alaams), if they were asked "Who did this territory belong to and what does the name mean?" They would have to say, "Let me go back and check." I think that a lot of people were getting frustrated, because everyone else seemed to be moving along in the treaty negotiations and Simpson seemed kind of stalled. That first feast stimulated a great deal of activity and research, and there have been several more feasts since. But this was one big one that they had, because they haven't had a feast for years. So now everybody is in doing research and claiming what is rightfully theirs. It was quite an awakening, and it is still going strong. The kids getting names had a big impact in the school. (2003)

Reading about origins - Pansy and Marilyn

I have used class sets of the *Queen Charlotte Islands reading series* with my primary students. Rose Bell, my sister, wrote the Haida story about how totem poles were created, and Paul White, my brother, did art for the book called *Haida Art*. (Adams & Markowsky, 1998) I have also used the Txamsen series, which is a set of bilingual stories written in English and Sm'algyax.

The kids were really interested in these stories. They want to know how things were created: how did different things originate? How did people used to make totem poles? Why did they do it that way? When I got the story that my sister wrote, I let them read it and make predictions about what would happen next. They made comparisons between what happened years ago and what happened today. In this way I hope that primary kids are able to understand history. These are very valuable resources for teaching them part of the history, who they are and where they come from. In the Haida story, it says that people came from a clamshell. Reading the stories helped the kids to comprehend and understand part of the Haida history. (Pansy)

I also used those readers, and the Grade 5/6 kids always ask me this question: "If we came from a clamshell, then what did God have to do with it? Did God make the clamshell?" When they asked this, I would always tell them that I'm not saying that this is true, I'm not saying that this is what you need to believe. I'm saying that this is what Haida people believe. I have said, "What your family chooses to believe is up to them." In Grade 5/6, we also study cultures around the world in social studies. I always say "other people in other countries have totally different beliefs about creation, and there is also a scientific belief about creation." We talk about Darwin. I have said, "Ultimately it is up to you what you believe, and you don't need to make up your mind right now, you don't need to tell me. There is no test. It is always your choice what you believe." I didn't want the kids to go home and then have their parents to phone and ask, "What are you doing?" I tell the students: "This is a belief that is out there." The kids are always interested. (Marilyn, October 2005)

Gift giving/National Aboriginal Day - Marilyn

The first year I taught in Simpson (La̱x Ḵgu'alaams) was the year that we planned our salmon feast; it was near the end of the year in May/June, when the whole school got into gift-giving. In the intermediate grades, I arranged for a weaver to come in and teach the kids some weaving, and my husband came in to teach carving. Each child in Grades 4 to 7 either carved a spoon or wove a small basket. We also did glass etching, and we etched First Nations designs on mirrors. With the grade 8s and 10s we painted First Nations designs on canvas with acrylics. I just used all the materials that were already in the school. Then, at the end of the year, the students got to give their gift away. In June, on National Aboriginal Day, we had big barbeques and a couple of fishermen in the community went out and got a whole pile of fish; and the staff made baked potatoes, salads, and the community donated other things: rice, or whatever they could. We had a big celebration. The whole community was invited. The school bought two big cakes and provided coffee and tea, so there was enough for everyone in the village. The students did an art gallery in the gym to display all the artwork we did all year. Then there was [First Nations] dancing, and then the gifts were given.

The children gave their spoon or basket to a parent or grandparent. But then we also made a whole lot of other gifts. We made fridge magnets out of juice lids decorated with First Nations designs, and we had dream catchers and miniature button blankets. The class just put all these small gifts in a big box, and then we would walk around and give these to anyone. So everyone left with a gift.

During the year, while the students were working on the art, I explained that traditionally gifts are given at a feast. We talked about why the chief would give away his wealth. He is doing it in order to provide for his village; he is showing everyone he is very wealthy. He doesn't need anything, he doesn't need all of this, and he is able to provide for them. When you are a host, you are obligated to give something to show your appreciation to the person for coming, for honoring you with their presence. When you go to a feast, you are acknowledging your host, or the chief.

The kids asked: "well, how come we have to give gifts (goodie bags) when we have birthday parties. When I have a birthday, other people give me things." I said: "Well, you are acknowledging and saying 'thank you' for coming, here is something for you." (2003)

Doing a Mini-Feast with primary students - Marilyn

We did a mini potlatch. The kids did their own songs and I videotaped the whole thing, and it was just awesome. Parents came and they brought all kinds of First Nations foods:

salmon, deer, fried bread, and berries. In the first term, we started the artwork and introduced the idea, we started learning songs and dances. In the second half of the year, we introduced storytelling. We hired Sam (my husband), and he came to the Grade 2/3 class, and he made up a song with them about salmon. Then they made little headbands with salmon on them, and they made a canoe and sang about salmon jumping, and once in a while they would all yell "*haiu*". That is what you yell when you see salmon jumping, and they would all start jumping around. In addition to working with our class, Sam also went into every gym class to teach the same two songs. At the end, it was so neat to see every single student singing the same song.

(2003)

COMMUNITY SOCIAL PRACTICES:
CULTURAL CONTINUITY AND CONNECTING PEOPLE

Teachers draw on the practices of the First Nations community to construct interpersonal relations with and among their students and, importantly, with students' families as well. This encompasses the infusion of practices of respect, caring, and other key interpersonal dimensions of Indigenous pedagogy.

Marilyn captures this essential aspect of her own and her colleagues' work, namely the knitting together of the generations, in the vignette "Dancing for the generations." Sociocultural theorists identify connections and exchanges among groups of newcomers and old-timers as essential in building the "communities of practice" so central to learning that is dynamic and continuous (Lave & Wenger, 1991). Marilyn elucidates that often newcomers must do what some old-timers can no longer do. In concert with Pansy, she sees that these newcomers can uniquely create spaces that engage old-timers. Consistent with the notions that kids and parents (as well as teachers) can both learn from one another, Bea notes in the vignette "Sharing stories and songs" that students are also able to help peers.

Nadine provides another example of enhancing learning by building on Ts'msyen pedagogical practices. In "Learning from the elders" she relates how her own attitudes, listening, and questioning practices affected elders from whom she wanted to learn. Mel's experiences in a village school "I'm thinking of it while learning how to learn it " and Cam's "Culturally based conflict resolution" identify that Ts'msyen practices have powerful implications not just for the content of what children learn but for their interactions with one another and their teachers. Mel also emphasizes that it is not just a matter of students respecting teachers, but that this respect must be reciprocal.

In each of these vignettes, the teachers describe how energizing their work is when they are building spaces of support and encouragement through song, dance, language, and story in ways that build on First Nations learning practices and relationships among all participants. These spaces include learners of any age, no matter their views of their abilities. The ways in which these practices could inform and enhance learning in the wider school and community will be explored in the final chapter.

Dancing for the generations - Marilyn

Our family/community dance group is not based in any one school, but we have students in the group who attend many of the schools in the district. Last year I was teaching at Seal Cove Elementary, and we had a multicultural day, and a lot of the young people in our dance group go to school there. When we went out and performed, many of the staff members and parents were surprised. A lot of parents were saying (to their kids): "Isn't that your teacher?" It was a really positive experience to go into the school where I also taught. The principal phoned and invited me, and said how much she wanted us there for multicultural day. Our dance group is getting bigger all the time. Last year when we did the multicultural day, we had about thirty in our group, and now we have over sixty, and there are still people wanting to join the group, and we have always said "yes, just come on out."

Wherever I teach, I get a lot of kids who want to join the group. When we go out to perform, it makes it easy for the teacher-on-call, because the class that is left is pretty small. Some of the teenagers in our group from when I was teaching at Lax Łgu'alaams (Port Simpson) are the ones who either attempted or were threatening suicide, or had lost someone to suicide. In the dance group, they found something that they needed and wanted to do, and it seemed it made them happier and gave them something to look forward to.

I think that dancing is so enriching because it has something to do with the identity of the child. We are always talking about representing something, like the Raven's dance with the Ravens. I always say, for example, I am a Raven and I dance with the Ravens. I am dancing for my grandmothers who have gone before me who were Ravens, and who started all this in our family.

I think it is because our grandmothers give us our identity, our crest, our history, our stories. They are all passed down through our grandmothers, and they stay with us, and I think we realize that, and we realize that that is what makes us belong somewhere. We belong to the Ravens, this story belongs to us, that song belongs to us, and then because I think that when the kids realize that, it helps them have a sense of belonging. I think that a lot of them didn't have a sense of belonging. Like me, when I grew up, I knew I was a Raven but I didn't know what that meant, because my family didn't really talk about it. When I married, I moved to Port Simpson and it was so much a part of my husband's family. They know all their stories, they know everything, they know their history and I didn't.

I think that for a lot of people who are raised the way that I was raised, without any background or without any knowledge, when they come to realize their background, it really gives them a good sense of belonging. I think that when the kids danced their crest they realized they are a part of something, and it does give them a sense of belonging. I think that it raised their self-esteem, and I could see it in the students that I had that joined our group. Their confidence seemed to go up, their self-confidence, and I think it had a lot to do with having that sense of belonging and sense of identity in knowing the history. I think that is what I mean when I say I am doing this for my grandmother. I knew that my grandmother could speak the language, but she did not raise her children to be raised the way she was because she wanted her children to succeed in the White world. She thought that that was the best thing for them at the time, and I think a lot people thought that. I think a lot of people thought that not teaching their children the language was going to be better for them, and it is nothing against her. She did not do anything wrong, she did what she thought was right. It was right at the time, but when we look back at it, they couldn't see into the future, they couldn't see what was going to happen, but that is what they wanted, for their kids to grow up with a White education, and not what they grew up with. That was a choice that they made. When I say I danced for my grandmother, even though she didn't raise everybody with the language, she was always proud of who she was. She didn't dance or teach her children to dance, but we are going to start here, and it is what she would have done if she had thought, if she wasn't influenced by everything else. This is what she would have done. I guess that is what I mean by "for" my grandmother.

Sam's (my husband's) family all danced, but in my family I was the only one. My mom's sisters would come, and they would watch, and they would say "I really wish I could dance." And I said: "Nothing is stopping you." Now in our group, now that we have moved from Port Simpson and are in Prince Rupert, I have two aunts and my mother who dance in our group. My mother would come for years and just watch and watch and watch, and she would be all excited, and at our last performance, I said, "Mom, I am bringing you a dress, because you sing when we are practicing, you know all the songs, you know how we dance, and you know there is no reason for you not to dance". So she said "Well, I don't know; I am so nervous." I said: "It doesn't matter once you are out there.

You are one of a lot of us." I said, "You don't need to be nervous." My mother-in-law said: "Priscilla, if I can dance, then you can dance. I am older than you. Go put that dress on." So my mom ran and put on a dress, and she is just happy that she is dancing with us.

We have my grandchildren, two of my grandchildren who don't really dance; they run all over the floor and go wild, but my oldest granddaughter dances with us. So my aunt's daughter, and her granddaughter dances, and so we have a whole pile of my family that is now coming out; and when I grew up, my family was never very cultural. They were not very cultural at all, and so I'm really happy to see it. The kids who are in our group that are related to me also go to Seal Cove School. It just seemed like it was a great big family thing every time we got together. These are my nieces and nephews and cousins. The family that Sam has here living in Rupert all joined our group, and so a lot of my family is now getting in and wanting to get in, so I just keep telling to come and hang around for awhile and eventually you will get in, and that is how it is nowadays.[70] (2005)

Learning from elders - Nadine

I had to teach myself how to work orally. I couldn't get up there and just speak from memory, from my heart. I'd have to have everything written down, because I'm not an oral person. My generation learned by writing stuff down and memorizing from paper; reading and writing. We lost the oral teachings at about the time of my growing up.

I have older sisters who were still learning orally and they always bug me about writing everything down and reading

---

70 Marilyn is also part of a smaller performance group that consists of only ten people. This group works at the Museum of Northern British Columbia during the summer, and gets paid for their performances. Three of the ten members are secondary school students. The audience at the Museum are primarily passengers on the cruise ships, with up to 750 people in the audience at any one time. The dance group is alse fundraising to go to the Smithsonian Institute in Washington D.C. for the opening of a Ts'msyen exhibit.

everything. They remember, whereas I can't unless it is written down. It is especially true for the language. My sister can just hear it and remember it. I think that is why my older sisters never graduated; never finished school. They weren't used to reading and writing like we are. They understood the culture and the language more than they did the English. They were still growing up in homes where Sm'algyax was the first language and the culture came first.

When my generation was growing up, we weren't allowed to speak Sm'algyax. It had to be English only, and I think that is why we got further in school. We started out in English, and they started out in Sm'algyax and Ts'msyen culture. With my parents working so much and traveling back and forth, my oldest sister grew up with my grandmother. She learned the language and while she doesn't use it as much as she should, she and my other older brothers and sisters can definitely speak it and understand it. The next down, Deryl, Mavis, my hubby and my brother that died, they can understand it but they can't speak it. Then there are the rest of us who are younger than them. We don't understand it, and we can't speak it unless it is written down.

Now that I'm no longer in school, the elders see me differently. I get a lot more information from them. Before, I was constantly asking them if I could record what they were saying for some course, and I think seeing me writing it down scared them. Now I don't ask. I just go and visit, and I sit there until they're into a subject and then I start asking questions. One person I just love listening to is Arnold Booth. He can tell you the origin of every word there ever was in the Sm'algyax language. He is just a wonderful guy to listen to. As soon as I get home, I write everything down; that's how I learn. I think we lost the ways of the oral teachings at about my generation. (June 1996)

I'm thinking of it while learning how to learn it - Mel

I am trying to think of ways to incorporate the language into classroom management. My first year was really difficult for me. I had kids there who were uncooperative. They were class leaders, and once they started, others followed. I noticed one day that when I went to the First Nations language class where the emphasis was on respect and responsibility and knowing who you are, my class calmed down. I just said to them: "You don't dishonor those who have gone before you"; and it worked for a while. However, I didn't have enough language to continue. Also, the Sm'algyax program is separate, and I can't really take stuff away out of respect for the two Sm'algyax teachers who are elders. I don't want to put them through more extra work. So I went out of my way to talk to my aunts and others in the village. I wanted to get some information, identify how I might respond to kids in the Ts'msyen way. There were a lot of interesting comments. I think what's happened is that there have been lots of gaps that people have sort of filled in, and it's all tainted somehow; the way we were brought up. Things have really changed in the village. The three Rs have replaced the traditional ways of doing things, and I find that the further we get away from the traditions, the more problems we have.

I have been trying to think about how I am going to stop that and go back to the other way. I think once I figure that out, it will probably work better. Whenever I do it, I always ask the kids to add their input. I like to see which way they are going to go, and make it their choice. It is really important that they do. A lot of times they don't make choices. The school is just there doing everything to them without telling them what it's for or what's happening. For me, it's almost like I'm thinking of it while learning how to learn it. (October 1996)

Culturally-based conflict resolution - Cam

I had two boys in my Grade 4 class who got into a fight. They were having a bit of trouble adapting from primary and making the transition from Grade 3. They figured the best way to solve their problem was to beat each other up. It just so happened that they were both from the same crest, the same clan. They were both Killer Whale, and that happens to be my clan. It occurred to me that this was a perfect opportunity to embark on a feasting unit. Those two who were fighting were embarrassing their clan. You help your clan; you don't fight with them. So they ended up throwing our first feast. I got together with them, and helped them prepare a little speech. They asked their whole clan to help. I explained that you feed them, you pay them, and in return they are going to help you carry out a feast that will feed the whole community. They did all the cooking, and sat everybody that came in. These kids in Grade 4 did it all in the right way, as it was traditionally carried out. At the end of it they got up and spoke about why they did it and what had happened. It worked out perfectly.

(June 1996)

DEALING WITH DIFFICULT HISTORY

In addition to celebrating Sm'algya̱x language and Ts'msyen culture with their students, teachers also spend time introducing difficult historical issues, such as residential schools and the impacts they have had on First Nations communities. In working with these issues, Pansy bases her approach on the importance of personal experiences and narratives. In the vignette "Talking about residential school with Grade 12 students" she emphasizes that she has no first hand experience with residential schools, and she always brings in one of the resource people on the Role Model Program to speak about their experiences. Marilyn uses B.C. First Nations author Shirley Sterling's autobiography *My Name is Seepeetza* (see "Talking about residential school with Grade 4/5 students").

Pansy's and Marilyn's approaches echo ideas in Chapter 2 about the nature of learning from elders; the notion that "all I have to share with you is myself, my experience, and how I have come to understand that experience" (Patricia Monture-Angus, as cited in Anderson, 2000, p. 21). They understand, from the stories circulating in their families and communities, that residential school experiences involving abuse and deprivation have created great trauma for many individuals who are still seeking to heal. The very personal nature of these experiences and the teachers' intense respect and concern for these individuals dictates that they cannot speak on behalf of these individuals or require their students to represent, in a public space, the experiences of people in their families.

In the vignette "Diversity and discussion" Pansy also illustrates how she carries this principle through in her efforts to help students develop skills both in articulating their own personal experiences and in listening with attention and regard to the experiences of their peers. Her observation that First Nations students appear to be more outspoken when they are in a class with non-First Nations students reminds us of Bakhtin's idea that struggle among discourses is integral to the development of our personal ideologies. It underscores the notion that First Nations studies and Sm'algyax language are important, not only in the education of First Nations students, but that they should also engage and include all students.

Talking about residential school with Grade 12 students - Pansy

When I was teaching Grade 12 First Nations studies, I introduced the subject of residential schools by using a story that my husband wrote about his experiences. I also used one written by my (adopted) sister Rose Bell (I have been adopted by her family here in Prince Rupert). These are in the collection *Residential Schools: The Stolen Years* (Jaine, 1993). We did research about when the schools started, and then the students had to research and do their own stories about their family.

They wrote brief stories about how someone in their family, went to residential school. Was it a good experience? Was it a bad experience? It is very delicate, and you have to approach it in a really cautious manner, because residential school affected people in different ways. There is physical, mental, verbal, and sexual abuse. You have to teach about general issues and not get into the essence of what happened in there, because it is a long term effect, and some never heal. It is embedded in their memories forever. It is an individual turning point if they want to heal and move on. The only way I can teach this in high school is in a general way: dates, locations, why students were taken away. Other than that, the rest comes from testimony from individuals, because I can't speak for anyone, they have to speak on their own.

I ask the students just to write a short essay. I am the only one who reads it. It goes no further. Some wrote of the tragedy of their own parents' life, and if the students were interested in pursuing the topic by doing more reading, I would alwaysrecommend other resources. But I wouldn't go any further in a class discussion because it is too delicate, it is heartbreaking, and it is difficult for some students.

I brought three ladies who went to residential school into the Grade 12 class. Two of them were home/school coordinators at a Prince Rupert Secondary School. It was interesting. Everybody has different experiences, but it was good to hear first hand what they went through. These students, right now, they know they are very lucky in the school system compared to when these women went to school; how controlling that was, versus the freedom in the current mainstream education. They were able to compare through their stories.

I also used the National Film Board video *The Circle Unbroken* that has a very powerful segment on residential schools. The students talk about how easy it is for them versus the olden days, the freedom they have and the love they have between their own family members, the bonding of their family, and how lucky they are. It opens up their eyes, and they realize that they live a really good life right now.

The personal writing, the film, and then the visits from the three home/school coordinators; that is what I did to finish off my whole component on the residential school for Grade 12. (October 2005)

Talking about residential school
with Grade 4/5 students - Marilyn

In my class, we did not go into the same depth as they do in Grade 12. I didn't share any stories. There was one page in one of our textbooks. One group of girls in the class decided that they would like to read the book *My Name is Seepetza* by Shirley Sterling, her personal memoir of growing up in British Columbia and going to residential school. The social studies curriculum recommends it for this age group, but in my class not all students were strong enough readers to read it on their own. The students who read it, at first they seemed really sad, that Seepetza had to go through this. They were saying, "The nuns were so mean! Is this true? Did this really happen?" And I said, "Yes, it really happened, she wrote this because she *did* go through it." We talked about it, and one of the First Nations girls said, "I am going to ask my gran if she went to residential school." She came back and said that her gran didn't go to residential school, but she knew others who did "My gran said there were a lot of bad things at residential school." I said, "There were a lot of bad things. I can't say exactly what happened, because I wasn't there; but maybe your gran can share with you."

Then, that was about it. I'm glad that they know about it, but I also didn't want to go into any of the court cases [where former students are laying charges against specific priests and the churches and Canadian government]. We just didn't get into it, and I thought they were just too young. (October 2005)

Diversity and discussion - Pansy

The dynamics of teaching Grade 12 when the class is made up of kids from a variety of cultures is different than when the class is all First Nations students. When there were students of Chinese and Indo-Canadian background, they contributed a lot through their perspectives and cultures. When I had a diverse cultural mix, the students were really outspoken. Everybody contributed in class discussions.

In an all First Nations class, it was quiet. It was very hard to get them to speak, to be vocal and to contribute in classroom discussions of any type, any topic. It was a challenge. I had a few outspoken students, but it was always the same ones giving their perspectives. To stimulate discussion, I used the example of the Nisga'a land claims, because this is something that kids in this area know about. I clipped out articles from current newspapers on the pros and cons of Nisga'a self-government. I clip out people's opinions, letters written to newspaper editors. I assign individual articles to different students and I say, "Okay, you do this one, you give me your opinion on it." To stimulate them, it has to be something that is current and in their lives today.

From this study of the Nisga'a treaty process, they learned a great deal about the land claims issues and treaty process in general. I didn't give them yes or no answers, and I didn't ask for theirs either. They will make their own decisions. They developed that understanding on their own. So opening up their eyes to different aspects of the treaty process was the goal. It was not my goal to advocate for one position or another; to begin to understand the issues of sovereignty and Indigenous rights.[71]

(October 2005)

71 British Columbia First Nations did not sign treaties with the British Crown (Treaty 8 in Northeast B.C. was an exception). Consequently, First Nations' legal rights to the land have never been extinguished. The B.C Treaty Commission, formed in 1992, is still working through these claims. The B.C. First Nations Studies curriculum gives substantial coverage to these land claims issues (Campbell, Menzies & Peacock, 2003).

ENGLISH LITERACY PROGRAMMING: CONNECTING FAMILY TO SCHOOLS

While loss of First Nations language and culture undermined nationhood, it also disrupted and sometimes completely severed connections with parents and grandparents. Residential schools and monolingual, monocultural provincial schools eroded pathways for intergenerational transmission of culture. First Nations teachers' classroom work, narrated in the vignettes referred to in the preceding section, inventively weaves in valued community practices of conflict resolution, oral communication, and interaction with elders. Their creativity is also apparent in their work with parents through the district English language literacy initiatives.

Programming that accentuates literacy in English is a significant component in the Partnership Agreement between the district and the First Nations Education Council. These programs, outlined below, do not always involve Ts'msyen curriculum and Sm'algyax language. However, in emphasizing and taking concrete steps to secure families' involvement, they are nevertheless building on important Ts'msyen cultural practices. Historically, formal teaching of English separated children from their families. Current initiatives, listed below, are designed to use English language learning as occasions for unification rather than divisiveness.

• Family and parent programs in early literacy. These programs include Parents as Literacy Supporters (PALS), Parents of Preschool Students (POPS) and other initiatives, which bring parents into schools over an extended period.

• Summer Read and Play Program. These are full day, three-week programs held at eight of ten district elementary schools. They are designed to help children in primary years develop and maintain literacy skills in a camp-like environment during the summer months. Parents are involved in reading with their children. Each group of fifteen students is assigned a full time teacher and teacher assistant (for photos, go to *www.sd52.bc.ca/fnes/literacy.html*).

- English Language Development Program. This program brings support to First Nations students through the Ministry of Education's English as a Second Dialect program funding. Eight new teaching positions were created to work with approximately 500 students. Special efforts were made to "incorporate First Nations imagery and to honour and affirm cultural identity" (First Nations Education Council & School District, 2005).

- Family workshops: Helping Our Children Learn/ *Limoomim K'abatgüülk dm Suwilaawksat*. These workshops include topics such as self-esteem.

- First Nations counselors. The district employs four counselors assigned respectively to the special elementary program (see below for description), one at each of two secondary schools, and one for students from the village of Metlakatla (which has no elementary school).

- First Nations family support workers are liaisons between elementary schools and families.

- Home school coordinators are employed by the villages to assist students making the transition to secondary schools in Prince Rupert.[72]

(For more information on each of these initiatives see First Nations Education Council & School District 52, 2004, 2005 Prince Rupert *www.sd52.bc.ca/fnes*).

In the vignette "Working with parents on literacy," Pansy and Marilyn jointly relate how encouraging parents to participate is rooted in First Nations practices and ideologies of generosity and respect. This vignette also reflects their respective collaborative roles as classroom teacher and district coordinator in supporting parental participation. Pansy clarifies in this vignette that children's interest and enthusiasm can stimulate their parents' eagerness to become more connected to what is going on in the school.

72 The position of home/school coordinator was intiated in the 1960s.

In the vignette "Developing local materials for English literacy," Bea identifies the importance of using vocabulary and illustrations that are familiar to First Nations learners. In addition, teachers incorporate Ts'msyen practices in workshops designed to connect with families. In the vignette "Teaching about social responsibility," Marilyn describes how Ts'msyen approaches animated one family workshop that focused on a provincially mandated school program entitled "Social Responsibility." These cultural practices help teachers position students and family in new and constructive ways that increase their sense of belonging and counter the negative dynamics commonly associated with the school setting.

Another important initiative that is not specified as part of the overall partnership plan between the First Nations Education Council and the district is the community school.[73] Roosevelt Park School in Prince Rupert – with a 90% First Nations student enrollment – is a designated community school, and this facilitates the coordinated offering of a variety of the programs outlined in this chapter. Bea describes how this arrangement supports the work of First Nations parents and educators in her vignette "Sketch of an inner-city school."

This chapter details a rich array of programs, activities, and human resources. The advocacy of First Nations educators and community groups in creating these is apparent. The advocacy work has a long history. The programs have been created in a relatively short time frame. Continuity and growth of this programming will require ongoing commitment and energy. B.C. Ministry of Education initiatives to measure effectiveness of education through standardized testing and assessment (measures on which many First Nations learners do not perform well) could quickly redirect educators' energy to a narrow focus on test scores. First Nations educators will need to be persistent

---

73 Community schools operate throughout British Columbia in a wide variety of ethno-cultural settings. These public schools receive extra funding to hire a staff member whose work is focused on building school and community liasons. This provincially funded position is separate from First Nations home/school coordinators..

in answering these authoritative ministry discourses in ways that affirm and sustain their dedication to Indigenous pedagogical approaches and programs. This issue is considered in the Chapter 10 on directions for the future.

Working with parents on literacy - Marilyn, Pansy, and Bea

MARILYN: The district has made it a priority to involve parents in their children's education, and we now have several programs designed to involve them continuously through the school year, especially in regard to the development of literacy (see *www.sd52.bc.ca/fnes/literacy.html*). PALS (Parents as Literacy Supporters) is for parents of Kindergarten kids, and it is continuous throughout the year. There are materials for eight to eleven sessions; each session is about two and a half hours. POPS (Parents of Primary Students) is similar, but it includes Grades 1 to 3. We are also planning to do FAST (Family and Students Together) which is for intermediate students. Then there are also the Helping our Children Learn workshops for parents of secondary students. Each of these programs is open to all parents, not just the parents of First Nations kids.

First Nations parent attendance has been very high, and part of my present job [as First Nations Education Program Resource Teacher] is to make sure the programs are running smoothly at ten elementary schools, including those in the villages, and the two secondary schools in Prince Rupert. I help the teachers and schools set up a calendar of sessions for the year that is issued to parents at the beginning of the school year so that they can plan and book the days ahead. I make up fridge magnets with the dates and brochures that show what will be done on each date. Many of the schools do the sessions from 9 a.m. to 11:30 a.m. in the classroom, with the kids present. Parents take off work to come. Some of the schools have chosen to do the sessions at night. There has been an awesome turnout. Our First Nations parents have been absent for a long time from the schools, and this is really, really working to get them back in. And they love it, every activity. At the high school, every parent who had a high school student who was First Nations got a personal phone call inviting them to attend. The parents ask really good questions, and are looking for ways to help their children. There is also a summer Read and Play for elementary students to help maintain the momentum through the summer months.

PANSY: In the Parents of Primary Students, I do an introduction or a demonstration, and the students are so eager to show their parents what they know and how they are learning, and the parents just love these sessions. The programs have been really successful.

At the beginning of each year, there is a district-wide or a regional training session. This year it was in Terrace (not Prince Rupert) so some teachers got together at their school with their principal and just set up their own workshop. It's pretty self-explanatory. The whole approach has really helped with relationships with parents in general. It makes them more at ease to come in my class and ask questions about their child, and I think a lot of them are curious about me. They were saying "I've never had a First Nations teacher teach my child before, but it is really good." It made more of an opening; the parents trusting me and having a good liaison, good communication. A bridge for communication is there so it is much more welcoming to them.

We did circle activities, different strategies for reading skills and a whole huge variety of hands-on strategies that parents could do at home. We have adjusted these to have First Nations content and we used the binder that comes with the training, but we have added First Nations inserts to all of them and the teachers are made aware of them. They use them. We have put them on green paper (so you can find them easily), and put them in the binders, so that is what teachers use.

For storytelling, it is First Nations stories that are being told, and teachers are encouraged to invite a First Nations role model in to tell a story. There is a locally developed book for math called *I See Salmon*. It has a First Nations drawing of a salmon. The flash cards have pictures of killer whales, eagles, seals, crabs, a lot of what the kids are really familiar with; things that they would eat or see around here. At the workshop we just developed for math, we had card games that encouraged counting for number recognition. Parents can play this game with their kids, and we gave every parent that came to our classroom sessions a deck of cards to take home in the gift bag. We had dice and a book. There is also a unit called "Print in our Community." The unit has photographs of all the signs in Prince Rupert that have First Nations arts on them so that the kids can recognize these and they see their community's artwork.

For some of the kids, their shyness wasn't there anymore. They kind of blossomed. You can see them blossoming right in front of their parents' eyes, so eager to tell mom what they could do. They are the teachers; they are the ones who show their mom and dads what to do. It builds their confidence, and I can see them beaming with pride. They are good sessions; a good way to communicate with First Nations parents when they often feel so uneasy in a classroom environment. Some of them think every time they come to school that it must be because their child is in trouble. But to go to the classroom in a positive environment can make them feel stronger and more confident in their abilities to go into a mainstream school. Doing it with PALS and POPS when their kids are young will build up their confidence to feel that they have a right to speak up and ask questions or find out what their child's learning. So that is a good opening.

I wrote the parents letters telling them what we are going to do, when we are going to do it. Many parents took time off from work to come, because they had the schedule way ahead of time. They were able to book time off work, and they did. They didn't stay for a snack or anything, but for the main content they stayed. If they can't attend, I ask them to please tell me and let me know. If they are working and they can't come, then please send a relative, or if there is no relative then I'll have the First Nations support worker buddy up with their child or my childcare worker will buddy up with the child. Not one child is left alone. They all have buddies. Even the principal came to be a buddy with one of my students.

I always call the newspapers up to give them an invitation to come and take photographs. I said: "Come and see my class. They were so popular last year". There are so many pictures of my class in the newspaper it is unreal. It makes them feel important, and it is a really cool thing to get their picture in the paper.

MARILYN: The newspaper article and pictures gave the program a lot of exposure. I think that a lot of parents are interested. We are just getting ready now to start Ready, Set, Learn, and that program is for three-year-olds; the little guys who aren't even in school yet. We are getting parents and the little guys together to show them what school is about, and giving the parents of three-year-olds strategies to help their child get ready for kindergarten and preschool. So we are organizing that right now. We are going to do it in the villages, and then here in Prince Rupert too. This is a Ministry of Ed program, not funded through the district, but I am one of the liaisons for the district, so there is continuity for the kids when they come into school, and so we can make sure there is continuity with the preschool and the kindergarten program.

Ready, Set, Learn doesn't have any First Nations content that I am aware of. But there is another program that the daycares in the villages use called Early Learning. I know about it because the preschool teachers developing the materials keep in contact with district First Nations consultants. There is also an adult literacy program in the village of Lax Łgu'alaams (Port Simpson) called Literacy Now that I am involved in and may travel over there for that. The classes are designed to help adults increase their literacy and their desire to read. Through this program, we might also be able to get money to build a library in the village of Lax Łgu'alaams.

BEA: Several of the First Nations parents who came to the POPS and PALS program expressed interest in getting on the school Parent Advisory Council. Usually the PAC members are all non-First Nations parents. But these were First Nations parents, and it was really nice to see that happening . . . that they really wanted to be on it. So I definitely see the change happening.

Attendance at parent meetings is a huge issue for most of our parents. Most of our parents are working in the canneries, so the reason I did the PALS during the first term is that they would not be working as much as they would in the spring. The springtime is herring season, and they get called to work. Rather than spreading my sessions out over the course of the year, I did one right after the other all in the fall. We had a pretty good turn out. I know we are not supposed to give the material out unless parents attend those meetings, but I don't know. I usually just talk to parents individually and have them come in when they can, and show them briefly how we use the materials. We do have a very high population of families on welfare and families that are going through crisis situations. Many of the parents are more open to coming and speaking to me if they can do so on an individual personal basis.

MARILYN: I totally agree with Bea, because if they missed the first session but you catch them later and say "at the first session this is what we did and here are the goodies that came along with it", it is more of an incentive for them to come to the second session. It is kind of like having a class and going around to all of the kids and giving them candy, and then saying "You can't have any" and then let the kids watch everybody else eat a candy or whatever. This poor little kid totally shunned and left out, and then punished because his parents couldn't make it. There are lots of reasons why they can't make it, like jobs. Do they risk losing a job that took them months to find? They finally get one and now to spend two hours at the school; I know it is important, but whether they are going to lose their job over that is something else. Some might be ill and they might not want to come to the school that day. They might have had a really bad experience the night before, you know, whatever.

I believe in giving a lot of second chances. If they miss one, then tell them to come to the next one and instead of saying "Well you didn't come. Your kid is not getting anything, if you want the materials you have to come." If I was that parent and that is what they said, and I was very shy to go into the school to begin with and then I was told "your kid is not getting it because you didn't come" then I would really, really think twice about going into a unfriendly situation when I am already gun shy.

I would do exactly what Bea is doing in catching them at a later date and building their confidence just one-on-one, and then the parent feels more confident to come in. I mean, we don't know the reasons, and we can't judge why they can't come, but we shouldn't punish the child by withholding something they really need. These kids aren't getting books at home. They are not getting the scissors and crayons and markers that get sent home with the other kids. They are not getting magnetic letters – they are lucky if they get food – and then we are going to say "you can't have it"; well, that is not right. The materials are already paid for. It is bought, it is sitting there, why let it gather dust until next year when a kid could be using it at home? If you can make it later, come and talk to me. That is just taking ten minutes out of your time, it makes a difference to that parent that could change their attitude for the rest of their child's school life instead of being really negative; but that is just my view.

(October 2005)

Developing local materials for English literacy - Bea

The learning materials for PALS have been adapted by the local curriculum developers so that they use local images. There is a published set of Aboriginal materials available, but even those wouldn't work in this region. We would need pictures of deer, not moose, and button blankets instead of feathers for illustrations. Administrators are becoming more aware of the need for these materials. We have always stressed the need to show our crests and our culture for all of the students. Our administrators are ordering more books with First Nations content, and I am now able to teach my block of fine arts with a First Nations focus, but it is also social studies because you have to talk about the meaning behind the art , where it started and how it has developed. Following are our alphabet cards.

First Nations Education Services SD 52 (Prince Rupert)

First Nations Education Services SD 52 (Prince Rupert)

Teaching about social responsibility - Marilyn

"Social responsibility" is a topic that the Ministry of Education requires us to work with. We think this is a topic that is important to work on with parents. The way we present it is by starting off with a speaker who is First Nations, who talks about the traditional way he was raised here: the respect, the amount of work they had to do; parents provide for a child and later children provide for their parents. They provide food, shelter; it was an expectation. Then from there we go into talking about our traditional feasts, and how everyone as a whole community has their role in part of the feast, and in the community there are also different roles.

First we talk about social responsibility in our First Nations communities, and then we talk about how we do it in our schools. We provide copies of the Ministry of Education performance standards for social responsibility. We also use the Martin Brokenleg video series and show the part of the video about generosity [Brendtro, Brokenleg, & Van Bockern, n.d.]. Then right after the speaker, we ask parents to put on chart paper the social problems that our children are facing today. We do a role-play about a conflict and a struggle between a parent and a child, and how they resolve it. Then the group will discuss what was effective. We ask them what they are doing at home, and then we look at all the suggestions that are given from all the professionals, like Martin Brokenleg. Then we look at what the parents are already doing and say, "You guys are on the right track. This is working for you." They share some of their struggles and what is going on with each other. That is how we do it.

One speaker related a story about when he was young and he was rebelling, and his parents would tell him a story they called "Raven's Wing." It is about a man who has a very poor sense of social responsibility. He is greedy and mean and abusive, and he hurts a raven. Years later, a group of kids are hitting the raven with a hockey stick, then the man tells them the story, and then all of a sudden the man is gone and he flies away. But that man that he is talking about is himself, and he has been turned into a raven because of all the bad things that he did, and now he has to teach other people. So we tell that story to the parents, and I think that the workshop helps parents to see that they are their own best resource. We want to help them to see that they can make changes for themselves or for their kids. Those workshops have been really successful. We do it for elementary and high school.

In the high school we had it in a different format than elementary, because we had larger groups of parents at the sessions. We had different centers (the story, the video, the role play, etc.). We had several things going on at the same time, and we broke the parents into groups and they went from one to the next. After they had rotated through all the centers, we came back together. The high school parents were just raving about it and they were just amazed at what they didn't know, and then what they did know at the end, and what they already knew before they even came.

There is always a dinner included, and after the workshop is over, we put out a whole table full of books and they get to take a book for every one of their children so that they can read at home. We bring books from the kindergarten level up to high school, and they get to pick a free book to take home for each child. We also have door prizes all through the night, and some of the curriculum resources – like a hardcover book about the salmon – are really popular prizes. First Nations T-shirts are also popular. When any of the staff win door prizes, we usually donate it back. These activities draw people in: the dinners, the door prizes, and the free books. I've been involved with this program for three years, but I think that they had it going one year before I jumped on board. (December 2005)

Sketch of an "inner-city" school - Bea

The First Nations population at my school (in the city of Prince Rupert) is 90%. We grab on to every program going, and I have got a great non-First Nations colleague at the school who has taught in a village and is on the same wavelength.

The kids at this school are amazingly resilient. Sometimes for them to even get up and come to school is a big plus, because of their home situations. But they do come; I think a lot has to do with the atmosphere of the school.

By the time they reach Grades 5 and 6, they are helping each other a lot. Not just in school, but outside of school. There was one girl who had to get her brother and sister ready for school because her mom either wasn't home or just couldn't help them. It was a really sad situation, but two of her friends would go there early and help her to get the kids ready, and then they would all get to school on time so they could get the breakfast; even if they were late for school breakfast, we would still find something for them to eat. Because Roosevelt School seems to go a little bit further in supporting kids. I think that the kids learn they need to support each other too. It happened a lot in my class. There were some who just couldn't be bothered to help others, and then there were some who just didn't want to be in school at all.

I agree that these kids are really great, just because of how much they try. They really try. They don't just quit. There are lots of learning difficulties in that little group, but they do try, there is a lot of support, and the people that work there really genuinely care. They have chosen to stay at that school. Some people do get bumped, some of the best and most caring teachers do get bumped.

We also have a really good afterschool program. We are so lucky to have the afterschool people and their programs. We had an outdoors program where we have a fellow who takes them out on hiking and camping trips. He tries to incorporate a lot of First Nations knowledge and surroundings. He is very dedicated. Everybody at that school really plays a very important part. It is not just teachers and administrators: there are the support staff, and there are the after school workers who are paid for by community school funding. Because it is designated as a community school, there is separate funding for that. The community school coordinator always has several big projects going with the kids: a Mother's Day project,

Father's Day project, and Christmas. Some of our kids aren't going to have money to buy their presents for their moms and dads. There is also a Nights Alive event every Friday night. It is like a dance. Kids are welcome to come. They have volunteers that show up to make sure that everything is under control. It works pretty well. It is just a matter of getting the volunteers. It is a very good project.

Our community school coordinator is not only supportive of our students' after school program, she supports the teachers on staff too, and she will always come up to you and tell you what events are coming up. She hands out flyers "This is coming up by the way. Remind your students" and she also helps with PALS and the POPS. We have these parents coming in, and she is busy welcoming them and getting the coffee and buying the pastry.

Then there is also the First Nations home-school worker. He does the phone calls to the parents if there are any problems. His primary role is to be an advocate for all First Nation students, and more recently Roosevelt also has set up a "hub." This is designed to be a drop-in centre for parents who cannot afford daycare, or want something to do with their kids. If they have a kindergarten child and a two-year-old they can drop in at the hub and participate in parenting sessions and crafts for their preschooler while they are waiting for the kindergarten child.

There is also an initiative through Success by Six, which is co-sponsored by the Ministry of Children and Families and the Credit Union. Now that the ministry is putting more funding into preschool, there is talk about setting up a preschool in one of the schools in the city. They looked at Roosevelt first. They are also looking at other schools, because Roosevelt now has the hub as a community centre, the community base. Our principal is saying he would like to get some Sm'alygyax resource people or some role models to do some songs and dances with the hub program. (December 2005)

SUGGESTED DISCUSSION QUESTIONS

1. The production of classroom resource materials is commonly considered tangible evidence that First Nations languages and cultures are recognized in schools. The classroom and community practices described in these vignettes are sometimes not associated with print materials. What other resources (besides formal curriculum) are teachers drawing on in constructing their practices?

2. How do the discourses of school-based classroom management programs compare to Indigenous discourses of respect?

3. What are some situations in your workplace where formal or informal curriculum relating to First Nations knowledge and practices would be a creative way to respond to educational challenges?

4. How might your varied positions as teacher, parent, and community member help you in building educational approaches that draw on First Nations linguistic and cultural resources? What skills and knowledge do you already have? What do you feel you will need to learn? Who are you already connected to who can support your work? What new connections would you like to make to others? Are there people whose work inspires your own creativity?

5. If you wanted to build new curriculum and programs, what steps could you take right away? What might take longer?

6. Do you know of projects in your own or other districts similar to those described in this chapter? Is it possible to get together with some of the people who have worked on these?

7. Review some of the key aspects of Indigenous pedagogies outlined in Chapter 3. What do you see in the vignettes in this chapter that corresponds to key characteristics such as working with elders, emphasizing personal, oral, and experiential ways of learning, appreciating the holistic nature and interconnections among land and people, emphasizing respectful and caring relationships?

CHAPTER 10:
LOOKING TO THE FUTURE

Identities are important bases from which people create
new worlds and new ways of being.
(Holland, Lachicotte, Skinner, & Cain, 1998, p. 5)

The vignettes in this book illustrate the dilemmas and
contradictions involved in building new educational worlds.
Teachers' identities and their ever-developing connections
to First Nations languages and cultures are rich resources in their
struggles with the educational legacies of colonialism. Feminist
educator Kathleen Casey reminds us in her research on women
teachers who are agents of social change that these are political
struggles. "Not only the state and its institutions are terrains of
political struggle; so is language. Even personal identity is an
arena of political activity" (1993, p. 158).

The vignettes collected here richly illustrate how identity,
language, and institutional change, the personal and the
political, are intertwined. The vignettes illustrate the ways in
which teachers act as powerful agents of change. In Anderson's
terms, the work of these First Nations teachers is an imaginative
and visionary component of nation building (1983).
Consequently, it is essential to acknowledge and situate the
documented educational changes within wider political and
economic contexts of Ts'msyen nationhood. Consideration of
possibilities for future educational change is also of utmost
importance.

THE POLITICAL AND ECONOMIC ARENAS OF NATION BUILDING

At the same time that First Nations teachers are developing
new educational pathways, their colleagues in local government,
health care, land claims, and economic development are dealing
with political, geographic, and economic considerations of
sovereignty. Structural changes in these arenas are essential in
creating new social worlds and more powerfully positioning

First Nations people to continue the work of building an ever-changing culture and society.

In British Columbia, where no sovereignty extinguishing treaties were ever signed, the B.C. Treaty Commission and First Nations are engaged in resolving longstanding land claims issues one nation at a time (retrieved October 5, 2007 from *www.bctreaty.net/index.php*). How these, as well as other major economic and land use issues around forestry, the fisheries, tourism, and the development of the international port of Prince Rupert are negotiated will affect the future economic livelihood of the region. At the same time that educators are working to build a new culture in the schools, local and regional First Nations government are working to build a regional economic base. Accomplishments in each world have implications for the other. Just as the Ts'msyen Tribal Council, established in 1989 to take up land claims issues, has championed educational initiatives, the local government and infrastructures that will come from successful land claims negotiations will be supported by and depend on educational strengths of community members.

EDUCATIONAL FUTURES

The educational programs negotiated, transacted, and documented here (as well as future programs) have long-range implications. As the teachers who compiled these vignettes enter their twelfth year of teaching, two areas are prominent. First, like other educators across North America, teachers are struggling with mainstream discourses and growing government demands for standardization and testing as measures of educational achievement. The second prominent concern is the expansion of the Sm'algyax language and Ts'msyen cultural materials and practices in schooling. Opportunities for all students in Grades 1 to 4 to participate in language programming is of special importance. This opportunity should be available to students in the city, as well as those in village schools. The ways in which Ts'msyen educators respond to these issues is instructive for others dealing with similar issues.

STANDARDIZED TESTING

Since Europeans first set up churches and schools to suppress First Nations languages and cultural practices, the supposed failure of First Nations students to complete mainstream schooling or to measure up to mainstream norms has been relentlessly documented. Successive programs have targeted First Nations students for remediation. Presently in British Columbia, the Foundation Skills Assessment (FSA) is administered annually to all BC students in Grades 4 and 7. It tests student abilities in reading comprehension, writing, and numeracy. Provincial Learning Assessments also are administered in all Grade 4 and 7 classrooms. The latter cover the subjects or cross-curricular areas not covered by the FSA. Additionally there is a wide range of subject matter provincial exams administered in Grades 10, 11, and 12 (see *www.bced.gov.bc.ca/assessment/*).

First Nations students' failure to perform at normative levels on these exams is a constant. Responsibility for failure is commonly attributed to parents, teachers, and students, and rarely to the institutional histories and practices in which all actors are enmeshed. Teaching to the standardized test to improve student performance becomes a tool for enforcing conformity (Kohn, 2000). Kohn further contends that top-down, test-driven versions of school reform have "turned schools into giant test-prep centers, effectively closing off intellectual inquiry and undermining enthusiasm for learning (and teaching)" (Kohn, 2006). Efforts to standardize, as Varenne and McDermott eloquently document in *Successful Failure* (1999), succeed in creating the very failure they are presumed to remediate. Efforts to remediate failure create more programs that narrow educational focus on measurable test outcomes. It is a vicious cycle in which students from minority language and cultures are the most common (but not the only) victims.

In this context, where considerable financial and educational resources are targeted on testing, the First Nations Education Council, district staff, and teachers consistently focus on the adequacy of the programs, rather than the presumed failure of the learners. They have creatively taken the emphasis on literacy and worked at ways of reconfiguring this to embody First Nations pedagogical approaches that incorporate strong emphases on listening and storytelling, as well as directly involving parents and community as program participants. In their Accountability Contract report to the Ministry, they repeatedly cite Ts'msyen culture and Sm'algya̱x language and parental involvement as essential in building literacy skills. Obliged to test students, they have reported scores for the district overall, rather than school by school. This takes the focus off of the individual classrooms and refocuses it on broader programmatic issues. This strategy could inform other minority communities, which must argue that building the curriculum around cultural and linguistic resources and practices rather than detracting from learning, in fact supports it.

The variety of pedagogical approaches outlined in Chapter 9 (literary arts, visual arts, dance, music, and participation in community events connected to food gathering and celebrations) are integral to curriculum; they are not "add-ons." Commonly, mainstream school acknowledgement of First Nations consists of adding on a dance performance or an art project. As positive as these efforts are, they do not penetrate deeper into those dynamics and practices of mainstream schools that exclude First Nations students. Along with involvement of parents and elders, genuine integration of community cultural practices has proven successful in increasing participation and school completion in other cultural settings such as in the U.S. with Black and Hispanic inner city-youth (Ladson-Billings, 1994; Regenspan, 2002). Including community-appropriate practices and knowledge in a wider range of schools might begin to address alienation from communities and families. Practicing respect and generosity, listening attentively to elders, incorporating traditional ecological knowledge,[74] honoring the contributions of all learners, and recognizing the potential for learning that can be

---

74　For more information on using traditional ecological knowledge as a basis for science curriculum, see J. Thompson, 2004.

created by drawing on a wide variety of community resources is a model that has much to offer learners and communities of diverse ancestries, including those from mainstream backgrounds.

BRINGING SM'ALGY<u>A</u>X LANGUAGE PROGRAMMING
TO ALL PRIMARY GRADES

As Bea pointed out in "Sm'algy<u>a</u>x for all the grades," Sm'algy<u>a</u>x language is taught from Grades 5 to 12 in all district schools. Only in the village schools is Sm'algy<u>a</u>x included in kindergarten to Grade 4. The B.C. Ministry of Education Languages Policy stipulates that all students will take a language other than English starting in Grade 5. This facilitates development of the curriculum for 5 to 12. Commonly, French, one of Canada's two official languages, is the language of choice. However, the Languages Policy leaves it to individual districts to select what language they would like to offer, generally in response to parental and community desires and interests. Each of the village schools in the Prince Rupert district employs fluent speakers and language teachers to work with all grades, starting with kindergarten. Offering Sm'alyg<u>a</u>x in primary grades in the city would build on the fact that the language is introduced in the First Nations Cedar Road preschool in the city of Prince Rupert. Language might also usefully be incorporated in the new pre-school Success By 6 initiative.[75]

Developing kindergarten to Grade 4 programming would require more personnel, as well as new resource materials. It would also bring this rich language resource to more non-First Nations children as well. A huge body of research on language learning and the nation-wide success in Canada of French immersion programs that begin in kindergarten attest to the tremendous capacities of young learners. Early immersion

---

75 Ts'msyen educators are now discussing how they might best take advantage of the new Success By 6 collaborative initiative of the United Way, B.C. Credit Unions, and the Ministry of Children and Family Development. (www.successby6bc.ca/aboutus/Partners.htm).

programs in Maori language for children in New Zealand through the Te Kohanga Reo (Cherrington, 2000; Smith, 1999) and Hawai'ian language in the United States are well documented (Keahi, 2000). Parental interest is key to the success of these programs, which begin in preschool years.

Indigenous pedagogical theorists (Aranga-Low, 2000; Armstrong, 2000; Nee-Benham & Cooper, 2000; Silva, 2000) reflecting on projects in their respective communities in New Zealand, Canada, and Hawaii note that momentum for these programs grows as links among language, land, family, and community strengthen, each feeding and sustaining the others. Teachers who acknowledge and honor these connections inside and outside of classrooms and schools are vital in contributing to this momentum.

WILAAY, WIL'NAT'AŁ [76]

The teachers who wrote and narrated the vignettes in this collection are fulfilling the expectation articulated in policy and theory that they would bring positive changes to education. Their stories make it clear that change occurs daily, and it is constructed in the development of formal curriculum, as well as through their interactions in classrooms and with their own and students' families and communities. The vignettes also clarify that change does not come without struggle. The abundance of creative programs and practices catalogued in this book were the outcome of individual and collective efforts over long periods of time: they did not happen overnight. These programs began with the historical commitments of community leaders to keep children in their home communities in order to maintain connections with their families, their language, and their culture. Over the decades, the energy and commitment to continue the struggle remains strong, as evidenced by the coordinated and collaborative efforts of individual teachers, parents, and community political and educational organizations.

The teachers' vignettes tell us a great deal about their creative efforts to change longstanding oppressive educational practices and to create new practices, which open up rather than foreclose their students' futures. In sociocultural terms, Indigenous teachers are strategically positioned (Davies & Harré, 1999) at the intersection of the variety of discourses (Bakhtin, 1981) articulated in the interconnected cultural worlds (Holland, Lachicotte, Skinner, & Cain, 1998) – school, community and university – in which they participate. These teachers have unique opportunities to engage in dialogues in a variety of professional, family, community, and academic settings. By virtue of participation in these intersecting cultural worlds, they are well situated to synthesize new educational discourses.

---

76 *Wilaay* means "to know" (Dunn, 1995, p. 109) and *wil'nat'ał* means "relations, family" (Campbell, 2005, p. 237) in Sm'algya̱x.

What we learn from these teachers is that change will come through a thoughtful and sensitive examination of past experiences viewed in the context of new challenges and new opportunities. We also learn that this change often takes place in very small ways, and that it can be an incredible struggle among often dissonant discourses of the cultural worlds in which they live and work. Finally, we can see from their stories that it is through their personal commitments and willingness to openly explore and tell about their varied identities and positions as teacher, parent, student, and clan and community member that they continue to learn and help others to do so. Vignettes collected here reveal that teachers orchestrate and mediate connections with children, parents and colleagues with care, diligence, tenacity, resolve, skill, and insight. The classrooms and communities they are helping to collaboratively construct are microcosms of the larger nation they are also involved in building.

APPENDIX 1:
TEACHER BIOGRAPHIES

DEBORAH BROWN. Deborah grew up and went to school in Massett, Haida Gwaii, where she was a star basketball player. She returned there after the teacher education program to teach in Massett. She later moved to Skidegate, and taught in the band-controlled school. She has set up and worked with support groups for young women, and has traveled to and taught in First Nations communities outside of British Columbia.

MARILYN BRYANT. Marilyn grew up in Prince Rupert, and traces her ancestry to her Ts'msyen mother and Haida father. She moved to her husband's Ts'msyen village of Lax Łgu'alaams (Port Simpson) when she got married, and returned there to teach for seven years. She also worked as learning assistance teacher. Since moving back to Prince Rupert, she worked as the Project Coordinator for the Prince Rupert Steering Committee on Aboriginal Homelessness, as a classroom teacher, and currently as First Nations Education Program Resource Teacher. She and her husband direct a dance group for youth. She is currently completing her master's degree.

PANSY COLLISON. Pansy is from Massett, B.C. Haida Gwaii. She lives in Prince Rupert with her husband and children. She is a functional speaker in the Haida language, and she has learned many Smalgyax phrases. She has her Master's degree in education (SFU), and is writing a collection of narratives about her experiences growing up with her Haida grandmother. She has taught many different grade levels, adult education, and First Nations Studies 11/12

CAMERON HILL. Cameron (Cam) comes from a family of teachers. He grew up in the Ts'msyen/Gitga'at village of Txaɫgiu (Hartley Bay), where he teaches intermediate grades. He is also an elected member of band council and has worked tirelessly to make it possible for all students to complete Grade 12 in the village. He attended Northwest Community College before entering teacher education. He is actively involved in creating curriculum resources with a focus on village life.

EVA-ANN HILL. Eva-Ann is also from the Ts'msyen/Gitga'at village of Txaɫgiu (Hartley Bay) and has been teaching in the primary program there since her graduation from the SFU teacher education program. Like Cam, she was at Northwest Community College for two years prior to entering the teacher education program. They began their family as they began their teaching careers. Rachel, their first child, appears on the cover of this book.

ISABELLE HILL. Isabelle's lifelong home is Prince Rupert. She was born, married, and has raised her family there. She is Ts'msyen, and a member of the Sm'algyax language program staff. As well as developing curriculum materials for the program, she teaches in several schools. For many years, she has also led an after school community dance program. She is a member of the district Role Model program, and has taught at the Friendship House. She is currently completing her master's degree in the SFU program based in Prince Rupert.

MAUREEN LAGROIX. Maureen is from the village of Old Massett, Haida Gwaii. She and her sister Deborah were supports for one another in the years they were in Prince Rupert enrolled in the teacher education program. Maureen returned to Haida Gwaii after she completed the program to take up the position as head teacher in the newly opened band-controlled primary school in Old Massett, where she taught for seven years. She now teaches Haida language and learning assistance K-7 at the provincial school in Massett.

NADINE LEIGHTON. Nadine was born and raised in the Ts'msyen/Gitga'at village of Txaɬgiu(Hartley Bay). She worked at the village school for four years as a childcare worker/librarian before entering the same program as Cam and Eva-Ann Hill. She works on curriculum development, and teaches Sm'algyax in Prince Rupert. Her professional activities as an educator working with adolescents are complemented by her work with the two babies she has had since she graduated from teacher education.

BEATRICE SKOG. Beatrice (Bea) is a member of the Ts'msyen Nation from Prince Rupert, where she currently resides with her family. Not long after completing the teacher education program, she took a job teaching in Lax Ɬgu'alaams (Port Simpson). She taught there for several years, commuting weekly, and then secured a position teaching the First Nations elementary program in the city of Prince Rupert. She currently teaches at Roosevelt Park Community School, and is very active in engaging parents in the variety of literacy and other community programs offered through the school.

MEL TAIT. Mel initially taught in his home Ts'msyen village of Lax Ɬgu'alaams (Port Simpson). He then taught in the Ts'msyen village of Gitxaaɬa (Kitkatla) for several years. He is very interested in computer applications in the classroom as well as in bringing traditional patterns of respect for the person into the classrooms and lives of his students.

APPENDIX 2:
RESEARCH METHODOLOGY

This appendix provides methodological background to the book. It situates this project in the context of other collaborative research projects between Indigenous and university researchers, and emphasizes the appropriateness of a narrative approach grounded in Indigenous pedagogy. It concludes with a section outlining the chronology and details of the present project.

THE NEED FOR COLLABORATIVE RESEARCH

It is regrettable that a great deal of research in Indigenous communities was done by outsiders, whose work distorted or misrepresented Indigenous cultures. K. Anderson (2004) and L.T. Smith (1999) comprehensively analyze issues of ownership and power relations in this research. They identify a number of historical power imbalances, and the importance of redressing these. Inequities relate to the relatively powerful positions of the researchers vis-à-vis Indigenous peoples, as well as to the privileging of Western ways of knowing. Positioning First Nations as research collaborators as well as researchers in their own right is central in creating both equity and authenticity. It is also critical that research methodologies themselves reflect First Nations ways of knowing.

Historically, researchers carried with them authority that came from their positions as paid employees and representatives of government, universities, or museums. On the one hand, they lacked intimate life-long knowledge of Indigenous peoples. On the other, research subjects who could not read or write English could not verify their written records easily.[77]

The power of Western ways of knowing was accepted without question in the world of academic science. Lives, cultures, and languages whose integrity were based on linkages

77 *See next page.*

and interconnections among individuals, families, communities and the environment (as outlined in Chapter 3 on Indigenous educational discourses) were dissected and categorized in classifications that followed the formats of Western natural sciences (Snively, 1995).

In the context of the Anglo-dominated history of research about Indigenous peoples there have, nevertheless, been historical instances in British Columbia where First Nations researchers were powerfully positioned. In the Ts'msyen nation, bilingual ethnologist William Beynon, whose mother was from Port Simpson[78] (Campbell, 2005; Halpin, 1978) worked from approximately 1914 to 1954 with elders from the region (Barbeau, & Beynon, 1987). Importantly, his publications, which comprehensively documented a great deal of local culture, history, and language, are collections of narratives. Each begins with the name and cultural/linguistic affiliations of the narrators. This narrative approach, rather than the more common ethnographic approach of categorizing data and divorcing it from the contexts in which it was observed, is an early example of employing a research methodology that is consistent with Indigenous ways of transmitting knowledge. These narratives are a rich resource for contemporary First Nations curriculum developers (Hutchingson & Harrison, 1992; Thompson, 2004), because it is consistent with Indigenous ways of communicating history, narrative was also selected as integral to the present work.

Carrying on this tradition of collaborative research and authorship are a variety of north coast projects, as well as projects in other regions of British Columbia, the Yukon,

---

77 Other abuses of power included the confiscation of masks, regalia, poles, and other sacred and valuable items. Recent successful repatriations include the return of a pole from the Ethnology Museum in Stockholm, Sweden. This was accomplished through the work of Louisa Smith, a graduate of the first cohort of the Prince Rupert First Nations Teacher Education Program. (*http://seattletimes.nwsource.com/html/travel/2002957077_webtotempole27.html?syndication=rss*).

78 His father was a sea captain from Wales.

and Alaska.[79] They connect Indigenous and non-Indigenous teachers, academics, elders, linguists, and researchers. They also attend to terms of reference defined by representative organizations such as the North Coast Tribal Council and the First Nations Education Council. The emphasis on collaboration and narrative methodologies in these projects informed the development of this book.

CO-CONSTRUCTION OF THIS BOOK

I first met the teachers who narrated and wrote the vignettes in this book when they applied for entry to the Prince Rupert First Nations Language and Culture Teacher Education Program. I was a member of the university-community panel that interviewed them as part of the admissions process. Subsequently, as faculty sponsor for the program, I regularly met and consulted with Debbie Leighton-Stephens, the faculty associate for the program.[80] I also attended selected program events. Thus, the teachers who wrote the vignettes and I were acquainted with one another while they were student teachers. However, I had no direct responsibilities in supervising their teaching or course work.

In the year before the student teachers completed the program, I conferred with Debbie about the desirability and feasibility of following up with the teachers immediately after their graduation. Debbie provided invaluable support and guidance in consulting with the student teachers and the district First Nations Education Council to negotiate the terms

79 On the north coast, these projects are documented in Evans, McDonald, & Nyce, 1999; Harris & Robinson, 1974; Menzies, 2004; Wuyee Wi Medeek, (John Lewis) 2004. Works in other communities in B.C. and the Yukon are documented in Cruikshank, Sidney, Smith, & Ned, 1990; Speare & Tappage, 1973; Turner, 2005; Robinson & Wickwire, 1989, 2005. In Alaska, the work of Lipka, Mohatt, & the Ciulestet Group, 1998 is significant.

80 The faculty associate is the experienced practicing teacher who organizes seminars, secures classroom placements, and supervises the practicum. Debbie Leighton-Stephens was a graduate of the first cohort of the program for student teachers, and is currently department head, First Nations Education Services.

of the research. The Council in turn provided letters of support and approval both to the Vancouver Foundation, which funded the project, and to the Simon Fraser University Research Ethics Committee, which administers policies and criteria for ethical research.

With approvals in place, I extended an invitation to each teacher to participate in a series of individual interviews. Nine of the eleven graduates expressed interest in participating in the project. While the documents describing the project explained that the objective of the project was to do a longitudinal follow-up involving yearly or twice-yearly interviews in the region, it was also explicit that volunteers could withdraw at any time. Moreover, if they wished to withdraw previous interview materials, this was their decision to make without prejudice. The first interviews began in the month after their graduation from the teacher education program, and focused on teachers' perceptions of their experiences, relative to their identities as First Nations teachers.

Not long after the first round of individual interviews, the teachers suggested that we hold group meetings to hear about each other's experiences. Over a nine-year period, we met in nine two-day and several one-day sessions. Attendance at these sessions ranged from a minimum of two participants to the entire group. Winter weather, demands of families, and – as the years went by – demands of jobs made it increasingly difficult to convene the group as whole. Individuals unable to attend meetings often sent written vignettes. I made a few trips to villages to meet with teachers for whom on-going travel was arduous and time-consuming. All costs of the meetings, including travel and district costs for teachers-on-call to fill in for the days when the participants were meeting, were funded from the Vancouver Foundation grant.

Our group sessions always began with open-ended informal exchanges about family and jobs. I then provided a short agenda to guide our discussions on the theme of bringing about educational change. The agendas were largely ignored; the group shaped its own agenda focusing on the variety of issues in education and community that were compelling and interesting to them at any given time. My initial request to direct attention to events that were challenging became a source of concern to some members, who felt that we were focusing exclusively on difficulties and not enough on successes. We subsequently reframed our discussions to share events that they thought they would remember for a long time to come.

The participants' attributed the positive and lively atmosphere of our discussions in part to experiences in their teacher education program. A key objective of this program is to support groups of student teachers in developing both an ethos of and skills in collaboration and communication. The on-site supervisors and instructors in this program highly valued these objectives, and worked to instantiate them in daily activities. It is tempting to assume that this group of teachers, because they are all of First Nations ancestry, would automatically become cohesive. But the day-to-day reality was a group of individuals with different family, village, and language traditions. The enthusiasm of the narrators to share stories and the richness of the discussions on which the current collection of vignettes is based owes a great deal to the earlier work of the group and its instructors in building an atmosphere of trust and support, without suppressing differences. Nevertheless, it is quite likely that there were times in our discussions when, for a variety of reasons, participants did not feel comfortable in expressing differences in perspective.

By the second year of our meetings, a number of individuals began to write vignettes based on memorable events. They brought these written texts to our meetings, providing rich material that stimulated more writing and narration. These written vignettes and edited extracts from the transcripts of our tape-recorded discussions provide the two main sources of vignettes in Chapters 3 and 6 through 9.

The vignettes use personal narratives to present problematic dimensions of authors' experiences with education, as well as the variety of their responses to the difficulties they perceive. Making the context and personal perspectives of the storyteller explicit helps listeners to understand that what the narrator learned or did in one set of circumstances might need adjustment in his or her own situation.

The terms outlined in the ethical review of this project guaranteed anonymity and confidentiality to the participants. Consequently, the first draft of this manuscript did not include references to the city of Prince Rupert, the Ts'msyen and Haida Nations, and the names of the villages or the teachers. When the teachers read the first draft, they unanimously agreed that they wanted their names and places of work to appear in the vignettes. However, in order to protect student confidentiality in the vignettes about particular students, the students' names have been changed, and the authors of the vignettes are not identified.

My work in constructing the book consisted of grouping the vignettes by themes (e.g., finding a job, interactions with communities, kids, etc) and organizing the themes into chapters. I then wrote introductions to these chapters that contain information that, in my view, would be useful in guiding discussion. The chapters on history were essential to fully contextualizing the narrators' experiences. In writing chapter introductions and providing historical and theoretical perspectives, I drew on my own understandings of Indigenous pedagogical theories as well as sociocultural theories of identity, discourse, and change. Also relevant were my experiences in working collaboratively in the development of several First Nations teacher education programs in a variety of communities in British Columbia. Finally, I was drawn to this project as an outcome of my personal commitments as a White Jewish educator. I was brought up in a family that highly prized its cultural and religious background, and at the same time encouraged me to learn from people of cultural and linguistic backgrounds different from my own.[81]

---

81   Beynon is the author's married name. Her husband's family is not related to William Beynon, the Ts'msyen ethnographer.

APPENDIX 3:
OUTLINE OF FEDERAL LEGISLATION REGARDING PROVISION OF EDUCATION

1868: A law was passed allowing proceeds from the federal sale of First Nations land to be used for "contribution to schools frequented by such Indians".

1869: A federal act provided that traditional chiefs could make rules on the construction and maintenance of school buildings.

1871: First Nations treaties led to the creation of the western provinces.

1876: The Indian Act implements its obligation, specified in treaties, to provide schools on reserves.

1877-1921: A series of treaties (Treaties 7-11) illustrate a subtle transition from aboriginal choice to Crown obligation. Location of instruction is limited to the reserves and the government is responsible for paying the teachers.

1894: An act of parliament established government authority to set up industrial or boarding schools, and gave Indian agents authority to decide on the transferring of funds to these schools, each of which was under the administration of one of a variety of religious denominations.

1920: The governor-in-council was given authority to establish day schools on reserves (Henderson, 1995).

APPENDIX 4:
SUMMARY OF SCHOOL BOARD MINUTES AND DIA CORRESPONDENCE

This appendix documents the seven-year process (December 1972 to May 1979) involved in transferring responsibility for village schools from DIA to School District #52.

• *January 3, 1972*. In a letter to the Board, the chief trustee (Iona Campognolo) wrote that Mr. Brodhead, district superintendant of education for North Coast District (DIA), has indicated some villages may wish to become part of District #52, and notes that "the Board will encourage action in this direction."

• *December 5,1972*. The school board meeting minutes record that Mr. Brodhead introduced Mr. Jim McCallum (A DIA official from Vancouver) who read a Band Council resolution from Port Simpson regarding amalgamation of their school with School District #52.

• *April 9, 1973*. Correspondence from A. H. Friesen, acting regional superintendent of education (DIA) indicates that the Port Simpson Day School could be transferred to the Prince Rupert School District by the following September.

• *February 22,1974*. A Band Council resolution from Hartley Bay to DIA providing a rationale for teaching Grade 9/10 in the village (which was in fact what happened).

• *May 30, 1974*. A memo from V.E. Rhymer, district supervisor, North Coast District (DIA), to Mr. W.G. Robinson, regional engineer, specifies need for classroom space and required electrical upgrading to Hartley Bay and Kitkatla to accommodate the potential addition of Grades 9 and 10.

• *March 18, 1975*. In a supplementary report to the school board from the Superintendent of District #52 (R.F. Lucas), there is a note that:

> The three Band Councils presented resolutions requesting that the Department of Indian Affairs and the Councils commence discussion with School District 52 regarding the possibility of operation of their schools by this Board. Further, the superintendent . . . asked the local DIA office for some of the data that would be needed (e.g., staffing and enrollments), but discussions would be required on a good many aspects with regional DIA officials and Department of Education officials preliminary to discussions with the local Band Councils.

• *July 25, 1975*. DIA approves a four-classroom addition for Port Simpson. Remarks on the proposal for approval indicate that the existing nine classroom school plus gym, library, and basement science and home economics room provides kindergarten to Grade 9 education for 297 children in the 1974-75 academic year. The Band wishes to have a Grade 10 program offered in 1975-76. It is proposed that the school will offer a complete education program from kindergarten to Grade 12 in 1979-80.

• *September 2, 1975*. The School District confirms temporary appointments to School District #52 staff until June 30, 1976 of eighteen teachers "on loan" from DIA and also moves that:

> A letter be written to the Band councils at Port Simpson, Hartley Bay and Kitkatla inviting a representative of their Education Committee to attend Board Meetings in Prince Rupert, advising that funds are not available from the School District for transportation to Prince Rupert, and that the representation would be on a non-voting basis, for the interim period September 3, 1975 to June 30, 1976.

• *September 16, 1975.* The agreement between the Government of British Columbia and the Government of Canada regarding the "take-over" of the three village schools by school District #52 was circulated for information at the School Board meeting.

• *January 20, 1976.* It was recommended at the School Board meeting that no decision be made on the take-over of Indian schools at Port Simpson, Hartley Bay and Kitkatla, until February 1976, that the regional office of DIA provide teachers on loan to School District#52 with the necessary notice, and that the Band Councils be contacted regarding the feeling of the villagers towards the take-over of their schools by this School District.

• *April 6, 1976.* There is a motion approved that the take-over decision be deferred until after April 20, 1976.

• *April 20, 1976.* There is a tie vote, 3 to 3. Motion defeated that "the take over be held off for one year." It was agreed that a meeting be set up with Department of Education officials and Indian and Northern Affairs officials in Vancouver during the trustees' convention in May.

• *May 11, 1976.* The School Board votes to request that the "special arrangement" be continued for the school year 1976/77 and that a meeting be arranged with M.P. Iona Campagnolo.

• *July 6,1976.* A memorandum-of-agreement between the Province of BC and the Government of Canada regarding the "take over" of Port Simpson, Hartley Bay and Kitkatla Schools by School District #52 for 1976/77 is circulated, and a motion is passed that the Board concurs with this memorandum-of-agreement. At this meeting the Board also confirmed the appointments of the teachers previously "on loan" from DIA.

- *November 2, 1976.* Letter from E. Hill to M.P. and Minister of State for Fitness and Amateur Sport Iona Campagnolo regarding the need for a new school at Hartley Bay (includes reference to the fact that they currently are accommodating grades 9 and 10) is introduced.

- *January 18, 1977.* A letter from A.H. Friesen Assistant, regional director education, DIA to School District Board #52 requests a meeting between Band Councils and the School Board regarding the disposition of village schools in Port Simpson, Hartley Bay, and Kitkatla. It was agreed that a meeting be held at the School Board office on Monday February 7th and that the matter of take-over be referred to the second meeting in February, at which time they agreed to continue with the same terms until September 1, 1977.

- *January 18, 1977.* A letter from the Kitkatla Band Council to the School Board advised that "they are agreeable with having one rural trustee from School District #52 as their representative, with the stipulation that one unofficial, non-active member sit in at both committee and open sessions of the regular School Board Meetings."

- *March 1, 1977.* Hartley Bay Band Council advised the Board that they are satisfied with the present arrangement of having one of the trustees serve as the rural representative as well as sending their own non-voting representatives to all future School Board meetings.

- *April 5, 1977.* It is noted in the district superintendent's report to the School Board that "Treasury Board approval was received in Ottawa for the calling of tenders for the construction of an addition to Port Simpson school."

- *June 7, 1977*: It is noted in the district superintendent's report to the School Board that "A contract has been awarded by the Government of Canada for the construction of the new school at Hartley Bay and tenders have been called for the school addition to Port Simpson."

• *December 6, 1977*. Positions for a vice-principal and a principal's assistant are approved for Port Simpson and Kitkatla respectively starting January 1, 1978.

• *January 10, 1978*. J. Bryant of Port Simpson advised that "the special arrangement between the province and the Government of Canada had been signed by the Kitkatla and Port Simpson band councils and had been mailed to Hartley Bay for signature."

• *January 10, 1978*. Motion passed: that the Board consider introducing the Tsimpshean Indian language into grades 1, 2, 3, 8, 9, and 10 in Prince Rupert Schools.

• *January 17, 1978*. Vern Jackson, representing Kitkatla, advised that the official school opening will be held May 26, 1978 and that the Kitkatla Band Council approved of the Tsimpshean language being introduced into the village schools. He further suggested that an advisory committee, including village representatives, be set up.

• *March 7, 1978*. Motion carried: that the district staff continue an immediate survey of the three villages - Port Simpson, Kitkatla, and Hartley Bay - with a view to introducing or renewing native language programs in them in the fall of 1978-79 if the survey so indicates and that during the school year 1978-79 a similar survey be conducted in the Prince Rupert attendance area.

• *June 15, 1979*. A new school building opened in Hartley Bay.[82] There is considerable correspondence dating from the mid-1970s that documents the community lobbying that was involved, including letters to Iona Campagnolo, the Member of the Provincial Legislative Assembly for the region. A number of the letters to Indian Affairs advocated not only for decent physical accommodation, but also for expansion

---

82 There were no doubt a variety of other arrangements in intervening years but researching documentation of these was not in the scope of the present project.

in order to accommodate older students through Grade 10 so that they would not have to leave the community.

• *May 1, 1979*. Motion: That Ernie Hill be permitted to hold the monthly principal's meeting at Hartley Bay on June 15 in order to participate in the school's official opening.

• *May 15, 1979*. A request was received for one additional teacher at the Port Edward school (just outside the city of Prince Rupert) for the development of native studies courses.

APPENDIX 5:
CURRICULUM RESOURCES AVAILABLE FROM FIRST NATIONS EDUCATION SERVICES SCHOOL DISTRICT #52 PRINCE RUPERT, BRITISH COLUMBIA

Campbell, K. (2005). *Persistence and change: A history of the Ts'msyen nation.* Prince Rupert: First Nations Education Council.

Sm'algyax Language Committee. (1996). *The Adventures of Txamsm Series.* Bilingual in Sm'algyax and English. Ts'msyen Nation and School District 52 (Prince Rupert).

Vol. 1 Txamsm and the Chief Kingfisher. From an original narrative told by Henry Tate. Retold in Sm'algyax by Verna Helin.

Vol. 2 Txamsm and the Children. From an original narrative told by Henry Tate. Retold in Sm'algyax by Pauline Dudoward.

Vol. 3 Txamsm Visits Chief Echo. From an original narrative told by Henry Tate. Retold in Sm'algyax by Beatrice Robinson.

Vol. 4 Txamsm Brings Light to the World from an original narrative told by J. Bradley. Retold in Sm'algyax by Mildred Wilson.

Suwilaawksa Sm'algyax (Learning Sm'algyax): a set of eight Sm'algyax language CDs and a guide book.

For more information on these and other resources, check:
http://www.sd52.bc.ca/fnes/pdf/resourcesbrocure.pdf

FIRST NATIONS EDUCATION SERVICES

SD 52 (Prince Rupert) • 317 9th Ave West, Prince Rupert, B.C. V8J 2S6
Tel: 250-627-1536   Fax: 250-627-1443
sd52.bc.ca/fnes

Curriculum Resource Order Form

Item	Price
Adawgm Hana'a Int Naksga Gatgadaa, 1986	5.00
The Adventures of Txamsm Series, 1996 ISBN 1-896462-13-8	24.00
The Adventures of Txamsm: Teacher's Resource Book	10.00
First Nations Role Model Poster Series (14 posters)	70.00
First Nations Theme Units for Early Primary, 2002 ISBN 1-896462-22-7	15.00
Gaboox, 1997	5.00
Gaxsoo : Canoes (Grade 5), 1997 ISBN 1-896462-23-5	10.00
Goo Gan Łaantga Aks, 1984	5.00
Goo Magn Sm Nii Maaxay, 1984	5.00
Keppered Fish, 1997	5.00
Kitkatla, A Northwest Coast Village, 1985	20.00
Łootm Smgan: Respecting the Cedar, (Grade 4) 2001 ISBN 1-896462-17-0	10.00
Łuutigm Hoon: Honouring the Salmon ISBN 1-896462-19-7	20.00
Łuutigm Hoon: Honouring the Salmon Teacher's Guide ISBN 1-896462-20-0	12.00
Molks, 1997	4.00
Na'ax and the Wolf, 1997	9.00
Our Smoked Oolichans, 1996	9.00
People of the Cane, 1987	10.00
People of the Cane, Teachers Guide, 1987	10.00
Port Simpson Foods, 1983	20.00
P'te'ex dił Dzepk: Clans and Crests, (Grade 2) 1997 ISBN 1-896462-18-9	10.00
Pts'aan: Totem Poles, 1996 ISBN 1-896462-16-2	12.00
Rachel Likes, 1997	10.00
Sm'algyax Dictionary (set of 2 books), 2001	20.00
Sm'algyax Dictionary, Student version (set of 2 books), 2001	10.00
Siipntu 'Nagyedu: I Love My Family, 1997	5.00
Sts'ool dił Awta: The Beaver and the Porcupine	5.00
Suwilaayksm Dzepk : Learning About Crests (Grade 7) 1997 ISBN 1-896462-24-3	10.00
Suwilaay'msga Na Ganiiyatgm (Tsimshian Series), 1992 ISBN 1-896462-00-6	75.00
Time and Change in Port Simpson, 1985	20.00
Tsimshian Clans and Crests Resource Book, 1997	8.00
Tsimshian Crests and Designs, 1997 ISBN 1-896462-15-4	12.00
Tsimshian Seasonal Rounds Poster Series	42.00
Tsimshian Series: Teacher's Resource Book	12.00
We Are All Related, 1997-98 ISBN 1-896462-14-6	15.00
Why There is a Rainbow	8.00

TOTAL ....

Shipping and handling extra

01/03/2002

REFERENCES

Abele, F., Dittburner, C, & Graham, K. (2000). *Towards a shared understanding in the policy discussion about aboriginal education*. In M. Brant Castellano, L. Davis, & L. Lahache (Eds.), *Aboriginal education: Fulfilling the promise* (pp. 3 - 24). Vancouver: UBC Press.

Abella, R.S. (1984). *Report of the commission on equality in employment*. Ottawa: Minister of Supply and Services Canada.

Aboriginal Education and Curriculum Branches. Province of British Columbia, Ministry of Education (1995). *B.C. First Nations Studies 12. Integrated Resource Package*.

Adams, D., & Markowsky, J. (1998). *The Queen Charlotte Islands Reading Series*. Vancouver: University of British Columbia, Faculty of Education, Pacific Educational Press.

Adams, D. (1983). *Haida Art*; illustrated by P. White and J. Markowsky. Vancouver: Wedge, UBC.

Anderson, B. (1983). *Imagined Communities*. New York: Verso.

Anderson, K. (2000). *Recognition of being: Reconstructing native womanhood*. Toronto: Sumach Press.

Anderson, K. (2004). *Speaking from the heart: Everyday storytelling and adult learning*. Canadian Journal of Native Education, 28(1/2), 123-129.

Anderson, K. & Lawrence, B. (Eds.). (2003). *Strong women stories: Native vision and community survival*. Toronto: Sumach Press.

Antone, E., Blair, H. & Archibald, J. (2003). *Advancing Aboriginal languages and literacy* [Editorial]. Canadian Journal of Native Education 27(1), 1-6.

Aranga-Low, L. (2000). *Grounding vision on the three baskets of knowledge: Kia ora ai te iwi Maori.* In M. Nee-Benham & J.Cooper (Eds.), *Indigenous educational models in contemporary practice: In our mother's voice* (pp. 45 - 54). Mahwah, NJ: Lawrence Erlbaum Associates.

Archibald, J. (1996). *Locally developed Native studies curriculum: An historical and philosophical rationale.* In M. Battiste & J. Barman (Eds.), *First Nations education in Canada: The circle unfolds* (pp. 288 - 312). Vancouver: UBC Press.

Armstrong, J. (2000). *A holistic education, Teachings from the dance-house: "We cannot afford to lose one Native child."* In M. Nee-Benham & J.Cooper (Eds.), *Indigenous educational models in contemporary practice: In our mother's voice* (pp. 35 - 44). Mahwah, NJ: Lawrence Erlbaum Associates.

Assembly of First Nations. *Assembly of First Nations-- The Story.* Retrieved August 20, 2006 *www.afn.ca/ article.asp?id=59*

Bakhtin, M. (1981). *Discourse in the novel.* In C. Emerson & M. Holquist (Eds.), *The dialogic imagination: Four essays* (pp. 259 - 434). Austin, TX: University of Texas Press.

Barbeau, M. & Beynon, W. (1987). *Tsimshian narratives (Vols. 1 - 2).* Ottawa: Canadian Museum of Civilization.

Barman, J. (1995). *Schooled for inequality: The education of British Columbia Aboriginal children.* In J. Barman, N. Sutherland, & J. D. Wilson (Eds.). Chap. 3. *Children, teachers and schools in the history of British Columbia.* Calgary, AB: Detselig.

Battiste, M. (1986). *Micmac literacy and cognitive assimilation.* In J. Barman, Y. Hébert, & D. McCaskill (Eds.), *Indian education in Canada: Vol. 1. The legacy* (pp. 23 - 44). Vancouver: UBC Press.

Battiste, M. (1995). *Introduction.* In M. Battiste & J. Barman (Eds.), *First Nations education in Canada: The circle unfolds* (pp. vii - xx). Vancouver: UBC Press.

Battiste, M. (2000). *Maintaining Aboriginal identity, language and culture in modern society*. In M. Battiste (Ed.), *Reclaiming Indigenous voice and vision* (pp. 192 - 208). Vancouver: UBC Press.

Battiste, M., Bell, L., & Findlay, L. (2002). *An interview with Linda Tuhiwai Te Rina Smith. Canadian Journal of Native Education*, 26(2), 169-186.

Battiste, M. & Henderson, James Youngblood (Sakej). (2000). *Protecting Indigenous knowledge and heritage: A global challenge*. Saskatoon, SK: Purich Publishing Ltd.

Bell, R. (1993). *Journeys*. in L. Jaine (Ed.) *Residential Schools: The Stolen Years* (pp 8-16). Saskatoon, SK: University of Saskatchewan Press.

Beynon, J.D. (1985). T*he Mt. Currie Indian community school: Innovation and endurance. Canadian Journal of Education*, 10(3), 250-274.

Beynon, J.D. (1991). *Career paths of Simon Fraser University Native teacher education graduates. Journal of Indigenous Studies*, 2(2), 49-70.

Beynon, J.D. & Dossa, P. (2003). *Mapping inclusive & equitable pedagogy: Narratives of university educators. Teaching Education*, 14(3), 249-264.

Bhabha, H.K. (1996). *Culture's in-between*. In S. Hall & P. DuGay (Eds.). *Questions of cultural identity* (pp. 53-60). London: Sage Publications.

Bolt, C. (1992). *Thomas Crosby and the Tsimshian: Small shoes for feet too large*. Vancouver: UBC Press.

Brant Castellano, M. (2000). *Updating aboriginal traditions of knowledge*. In G.S Dei, B. Hall,& D.G. Rosenberg, (Eds.), *Indigenous knowledge in global contexts: Multiple readings of our world*, (21-36). Toronto: University of Toronto Press.

Brant Castellano, M., Davis, L, and Lahache, L. (2000). *Introduction.* In M. Brant Castellano, L. Davis, & L. Lahache (Eds.), *Aboriginal education: Fulfilling the promise* (pp. xi - xviii). Vancouver: UBC Press.

Brendtro, L., Brokenleg, M., Van Bockern, S. (n.d.). *Reclaiming youth at risk* [3 video set and guide]. *www.solution-tree.com/Public/Media.aspx?ShowDetail=true&ProductID=VI F029* (retrieved November 3, 2007).

Cajete, G. (1999). *Igniting the sparkle: An Indigenous science education model.* Skyand, NC: Kivaki Press.

Cajete, G. (2000). *Indigenous knowledge: The Pueblo metaphor of Indigenous Education.* In M. Battiste (Ed.), *Reclaiming Indigenous voice and vision* (pp. 181 - 191). Vancouver: UBC Press.

Calliou, S. (1995). *Peacekeeping actions at home: A medicine wheel model for a peacekeeping pedagogy.* In M. Battiste & J. Barman (Eds.), *First Nations education in Canada: The circle unfold* (pp. 47 - 72). Vancouver: UBC Press.

Campbell, K. (1984). *Hartley Bay, B.C.: A history.* In M. Seguin (Ed.), *The Tsimshian: Images of the past; views for the present* (pp. 3 - 26). Vancouver: UBC Press.

Campbell, K. (2005). *Persistence and change: A history of the Ts'msyen Nation.* Prince Rupert, BC: Ts'msyen Nation and School Disctrict 52, Prince Rupert.

Campbell, K., Menzies, C., & Peacock, B. (2003). *B.C. First Nations Studies.* Vancouver: Pacific Educational Press.

Casey, K. (1993). *I answer with my life: Life histories of women teachers working for social change.* New York: Routledge.

Cherrington, K. (2000). *Building a child-centered model: "An Indigenous model must look to the future."* In M. Nee-Benham & J. Cooper (Eds.), *Indigenous educational models in contemporary practice: in our mother's voice* (pp. 29 - 34). Mahwah, NJ: Lawrence Erlbaum.

Clarke, J. (2006). *Métis residential school survivors excluded from deal.* Aboriginal Times, 11(5), 26.

Collison, A. (1993). *Healing myself through our Haida traditional customs.* in L. Jaine (Ed.) *Residential Schools: The stolen years.* (pp 35-42) Saskatoon, SK: University of Saskatchewan Press.

Cruikshank, J., Sidney, A. Smith, K., & Ned, A. (1990). *Life lived like a story: Life stories of three Yukon Native elders.* Vancouver: UBC Press.

Curwen Doig, L. (2003). *A missing link: Between traditional Aboriginal education and the western system of education.* Canadian Journal of Native Education, 27(2), 144-160.

Davies, B. & Harré, R. (1999). *Positioning: The discursive production of selves.* Retrieved November 3, 2007 from *www.massey.ac.nz/~Alock/position.htm*

Department of Justice, Canada. (2005). *Healing the past: Addressing the legacy of physical and sexual abuse in Indian residential schools.* Retrieved November 3, 2007 from *www.justice.gc.ca/en/dept/pub/dig/healing.htm*

Duff, W. (1964). *The Indian history of British Columbia: Vol. 1. The impact of the White man.* Victoria, BC: Provincial Museum of Natural History and Anthropology.

Dunn, J. (1995). *Sm'algyax: A reference dictionary and grammar for the coast Tsimshian language.* Seattle, WA: University of Washington Press.

Emerson, C. & Holquist, M. (Eds.). *Glossary. The dialogic imagination: Four essays by M.M. Bakhtin* (p.p. 423 - 434). Austin, TX: University of Texas Press.

Evans, M., McDonald, J., & Nyce, D. (1999). *Acting across boundaries in Aboriginal curriculum development: Examples from Northern British Columbia. Canadian Journal of Native Education*, 23(2), 190-208.

First Nations Education Council & School District 52 (Prince Rupert). (2004). *Suwilaawksa Ts'msyen A wil Ho'yaxst Dm Sagayt Hakhalelst/First Nations education partnership agreement: Annual report* 2003-2004. Retrieved November 5, 2005 from *www.sd52.bc.ca*

First Nations Education Council & School District 52 (Prince Rupert). (2005). *Sagayt suwilaawksa Galts'ap/A community of learners. Partnership Agreement.* Retrieved November 5, 2005 from *www.sd52.bc.ca/fnes/pdf/annual%20report2005-05.pdf*

Fournier, S., & Crey, E. (1997). *Stolen from our embrace: The abduction of First Nations children and the restoration of Aboriginal communities.* Vancouver: Douglas & McIntyre.

Freire, P. (1970). *Pedagogy of the oppressed.* New York: The Seabury Press.

Gardner, E. (2000). *First Nations House of Learning: A continuity of transformation.* In M. Brant Castellano, L. Davis, & L. Lahache (Eds.), *Aboriginal education: Fulfilling the promise* (pp. 190 - 209). Vancouver: UBC Press.

Gillborn, D. (1995). *Racism and anti-racism in real schools.* Philadelphia: Open University Press.

Glavin, T., & Former students of St. Mary's. (2002). *Amongst God's own: The enduring legacy of St. Mary's Mission.* Mission, BC: Longhouse Publishing.

Gordon, J. (2000). *The color of teaching.* New York: Routledge.

Government of Canada (1986). *Employment equity act.* Ottawa: Queen's Printer.

Haig-Brown, C. (1988). *Resistance and renewal: Surviving the Indian residential school.* Vancouver: Tillacum Library.

Hall, S. (1996). *Who needs identity?* In S. Hall & P. du Gay (Eds.), *Questions of cultural identity* (pp. 1 - 17). London: Sage Publications.

Halpin, M. (1978). *William Beynon, ethnographer.* In M. Liberty (Ed.), *American Indian intellectuals* (pp. 141 - 156). New York: West Publishing Company.

Hampton, E. (1995). *Towards a redefinition of Indian education.* In M. Battiste & J. Barman (Eds.), *First Nations education in Canada: The circle unfolds* (pp. 5 - 46). Vancouver: UBC Press.

Hampton, E. (2000). *First Nations-controlled university education in Canada.* In M. Brant Castellano, L. Davis, & L. Lahache (Eds.), *Aboriginal education: Fulfilling the promise* (pp. 208 - 223). Vancouver: UBC Press.

Hanks, W.F. (1991). *Forward.* In J. Lave & E. Wenger (Eds.), *Situated learning: Legitimate peripheral participation* (pp. 13 - 24). Cambridge, UK: Cambridge University Press.

Harris, K. & Robinson F. (1974). *Visitors who never left: The origin of the people of Damlehamid.* Vancouver: UBC Press.

Hartley Bay School (1996,1997). *Hartley Bay School: Presents to you [Six primary grade readers in English and Sm'algyax].* (Available from Hartley Bay School, School District #52, First Nations Education Services, 317 9th Avenue West, Prince Rupert, BC, V8J 2S6.)

Hawthorn, H., Tremblay, M., Vallee, F., & Ryan, J. (1967). *A survey of contemporary Indians of Canada: Economic, political, educational needs and policies (Vol. 2).* Ottawa, ON: Indian Affairs Branch.

Henderson, J.Y. (1995). *Treaties and Indian education. In M. Battiste & J. Barman* (Eds.), *First Nations education in Canada: The circle unfolds* (pp. 245 - 261). Vancouver: UBC Press.

Henze, R., & Vanette, L. (1993). *To walk in two worlds--or more? Challenging a common metaphor of Native education.* Anthropology and Education Quarterly, 24(2), 116-134.

Holland, D., Lachicotte, W., Skinner, D., & Cain, C. (1998). *Identity and agency in cultural worlds.* Cambridge, MS: Harvard University Press.

Holland, D., & Lave, J., (Eds.). (2000). *History in person: Enduring struggles, contentious practice, intimate identities.* Santa Fe, NM: School of American Research Press.

hooks, b. (1994). *Teaching to transgress: Education as the practice of cultural freedom.* New York: Routledge.

Horton, R., Trerise T., Gale, F., & Carboni, J. (1994). *Kitkatla — A northwest coast village: A grade three social studies project.* (Available from Hartley Bay School, School District #52, First Nations Education Services, 317 9th Avenue West, Prince Rupert, BC, V8J 2S6.)

Hutchingson, V., & Harrison, D. (1992). *The Ts'msyen language series, Suwilaay'msga Na G a'niiyatgm. (Vols 1 - 7).* (Available from Hartley Bay School, School District #52, First Nations Education Services, 825 Conrad Street, Prince Rupert, BC, V8J 2M9.)

Jaine, L. (Ed.). (1993). *Residential schools: The stolen years.* Saskatoon, SK: University of Saskatchewan Press.

Keahi, S. (2000). *Advocating for a stimulating language based education: "If you don't learn your language where can you go home to?"* In M. Nee-Benham & J. Cooper (Eds.), *Indigenous educational models in contemporary practice: In our mother's voice* (pp. 55 - 60). Mahwah, NJ: Lawrence Erlbaum.

Keeshig-Tobias, L. (2003). *Of hating, hurting and coming to terms with the English language. Canadian Journal of Native Education,* 27(1), 89-100.

Kenny, C., & Archibald, J. (2000). *Q'epethet ye Mestiyexw, A gathering of the people. Canadian Journal of Native Education,* 24(1), 1-5.

Kirkness, V. (1989). *Aboriginal languages in Canada: From confusion to certainty. Journal of Indigenous Studies*, 1(2), 97-103.

Kirkness, V. (1998). *The critical state of Aboriginal languages in Canada. Canadian Journal of Native Education*, 22(9), 93-104.

Kirkness, V. (1999). *Native Indian teachers: A key to progress. Canadian Journal of Native Education*, 23(1), 57-63.

Kirkness, V., & Bowman, S. (1992). *First Nations and schools: Triumphs and struggles.* Toronto: Canadian Education Association.

Kleinfeld, J. (1972). *Effective teachers of Indian and Eskimo high school students.* Fairbanks, AK: Institute of Social, Economic, and Government Research, University of Alaska.

Kohn, A. (2000). *The case against standardized testing: Raising the scores, ruining the schools.* Portsmouth, NH: Heinemann.

Kohn, A. (2006). *Our fixation on test scores is killing good teaching methods.* [Media release]. Vancouver: Vancouver School Board. Retrieved November 3, 2007 from *www.vsb.bc.ca/districtinfo/districtpublication/newsmedia/200 61011.htm*

Kress, G. (1989). *Linguistic processes in sociocultural practice.* Oxford: Oxford University Press.

Ladson-Billings, G. (1994). *The dreamkeepers: Successful teachers of African American children.* San Francisco: Jossey-Bass.

Lave, J., & Wenger, E. (1991). *Situated learning: Legitimate peripheral participation.* New York: University of Cambridge Press.

Lipka, J., Mohatt, G., & the Ciulestet Group. (1998). *Transforming the culture of the schools: Yup'ik Eskimo examples.* Mahwah, NJ: Lawrence Erlbaum Associates.

Lomawaima, K.T. (1994). *They called it prairie light: The story of the Chilocco Indian School.* Lincoln, NE: University of Nebraska Press.

MacIvor, M. (1995). *Redefining science education for Aboriginal students.* In M. Battiste & J. Barman (Eds.). *First Nations education in Canada: The circle unfolds* (pp. 73-98). Vancouver: UBC Press.

McCarthy, C. (1990). *Race and curriculum: Social inequality and the theories of politics of difference in contemporary research on schooling.* New York: The Falmer Press.

Medicine, B. (1987). *My elders tell me.* In J. Barman, Y. Hébert, & D. McCaskill (Eds.), *Indian education in Canada: Vol. 2. The challenge* (pp.142-152). Vancouver: UBC Press.

Menzies, C. (2004). *Putting words into action: Negotiating collaborative research in Gitxaala. Canadian Journal of Native Education,* 28(1/2), 15-33.

Menzies, C., Q'um Q'um xiiem, Archibald, J., & Hingaroa Smith, G. (2004). *Transformational sites of Indigenous education [Editorial]. Canadian Journal of Native Education,* 28(1/2), 1-7.

Mulgrew, I. (2006, July 17). *Courts will weigh offers to abused Native students. Vancouver Sun,* pp. B1, B4.

National Film Board of Canada. (1998). *The circle unbroken.* Montreal, Québec.

National Indian Brotherhood. (1972). *Indian control of Indian education.* (Available from the National Indian Brotherhood, Ottawa, Ontario.)

Nee-Benham, M. & Cooper, J. (2000). (Eds.) *Indigenous educational models in contemporary practice: In our mother's voice.* Mahwah, NJ: Lawrence Erlbaum Associates.

Neylan, S. (2003). *The heavens are changing: Nineteenth century Protestant missions and Tsimshian Christianity.* Montreal: McGill-Queen's University Press.

Osler, A. (1997). *The education and careers of black teachers: Changing identities, changing lives.* Philadelphia: Open University Press.

Paulsen, R.L. (2003). *Native literacy: A living language. Canadian Journal of Native Education,* 27(1), 23-28.

Phillips, S. (1983). *The invisible culture: Communication in classroom and community on the Warm Springs Indian reservation.* Prospect Heights, IL: Waveland Press.

Regenspan, B. (2002). *Parallel practices: Social justice focused teacher education and the elementary school classroom.* New York: Peter Lang.

Robinson, H. & Wickwire, W. (1989). *Write it on your heart: The epic world of an Okanagan storyteller.* Vancouver: Talonbooks.

Robinson, H. & Wickwire, W. (2005). *Living by stories: A journey of landscape and memory.* Vancouver: Talonbooks.

Royal Commission on Aboriginal Peoples (RCAP). (1996). *Report of the royal commission on Aboriginal peoples: Vol. 3. Gathering strength.* Ottawa: Canada Communication Group.

Scollon, R. & Scollon, S. (1981). *Narrative, literacy and face in interethnic communication.* Norwood, NJ: Ablex Publishing Corporation.

Secwepemc Cultural Education Society, (2000). *Behind closed doors: Stories from the Kamloops Indian residential school.* Penticton, BC: Theytus Books.

Silva, K. (2000). *Revitalizing culture and language: "Returning to the Aina."* In M. Nee-Benham & J. Cooper (Eds.), *Indigenous educational models in contemporary practice: In our mother's voice* (pp. 71-80). Mahwah, NJ: Lawrence Erlbaum Associates.

Smith, G.H. (2000). *Protecting and respecting Indigenous knowledge.* In M. Battiste (Ed.), *Reclaiming Indigenous voice and vision* (pp. 209-224). Vancouver: UBC Press.

Smith, L. Tuhiwai. (1999). *Decolonizing methodologies: Research and Indigenous peoples.* London: Zed Books.

Snively, G. (1995). *Bridging traditional science and western science in the multicultural classroom.* In G. Snively & A. MacKinnon (Eds.), *Thinking globally about mathematics and science education* (pp. 1-24). Vancouver: Centre for the Study of Curriculum & Instruction, University of British Columbia.

Speare, J. & Tappage, A. (1973). *The days of Augusta.* Vancouver: J.J. Douglas.

Stairs, A. (1993). *Learning processes and teaching roles in Native education: Cultural base and cultural brokerage.* In S. Morris, K. McLeod., & M. Danesi (Eds.), *Aboriginal languages and education: The Canadian experience* (pp. 85-102). Oakville, ON: Mosaic Press.

Sterling, S. (1992). *My name is Seepeetza.* Vancouver: Douglas & McIntyre.

Sterling, S. (2002). *Yetko and Sophie: Nlakapamux cultural professors. Canadian Journal of Native Education*, 26(1), 4-10.

Thiessen, D., Bascia, N., & Goodson, I. (Eds.) (1996). *Making a difference about difference: The lives and careers of racial minority immigrant teachers.* Toronto: Garamond Press.

Thompson, J. (2004). *Traditional plant knowledge of the Tsimshian curriculum: Keeping knowledge in the community.* Canadian Journal of Native Education, 28(1/2), 61-65. Retrieved November 3, 2007 from *www.ecoknow.ca/journal/61.html*

Toulouse, I. (2003). *Transference of concepts from Ojibwe into English contexts.* Canadian Journal of Native Education, 27(1), 84-88.

Tsimshian Chiefs. (1992). *Suwilaay'msga Na Ga'niiyatgm/ Teachings of our grandfathers.* (Vols. 1 - 6). Prince Rupert: BC: First Nations Advisory Council of School District #52. (Available from, School District #52, First Nations Education Services, 9th Avenue West, Prince Rupert, BC, V8J 2S6.)

Turner, N. (2005). *The earth's blanket: Traditional teachings for sustainable living.* Vancouver: Douglas & McIntyre.

Varenne, H. & McDermott, R. (1999). *Successful failure: The school that America builds.* Boulder, CO: Westview Press.

Wenger, E. (1998). *Communities of practice: Learning, meaning and identity.* New York: Cambridge University Press.

Williams, L. & Wyatt, J. (1987). *Training Indian teachers in a community setting: The Mount Currie Lil'wat programme.* In J. Barman, Y. Hébert, & D. McCaskill (Eds.), *Indian education in Canada: Volume 2. The challenge* (pp. 210-227). Vancouver: UBC Press.

Wuyee Wi Medeek (John Lewis). (2004). *Forests for the Future: The view from Gitkxaala. Canadian Journal of Native Education*, 28(1/2), 8-14.

Wyatt, J.D. (1977). *Self-determination through education: A Canadian Indian Example. Phi Delta Kappan*, (Jan.), 405-408.

Wyatt, J.D. (1978/79). *Native involvement in curriculum development: The native teacher as cultural broker.* Interchange, (8), 7-28.

Young, M. (2003). *Anishinabemowin: A way of seeing the world reclaiming my identity. Canadian Journal of Native Education,* 27(1), 101-107.

INDEX

C

D

H

I

J

K

V

W

Y